To my parents, Navneet Shergill and Siddharth Dixit

None of this would have been possible without your unwavering love and support. Thank you for planting the seed of giving in my mind and nurturing it with care. Your constant reminders that words of inspiration hold the power to change the world have always stayed with me.

And to my grandparents, who co-founded *GyaanJyoti*—a guiding light for economically underprivileged girls in North India.

"HOW WONDERFUL IT IS THAT
NOBODY NEED WAIT A SINGLE
MOMENT BEFORE STARTING TO
IMPROVE THE WORLD "

Anne Frank

ASK ME WHY

I wrote this book

School and Stories: Every Girl Deserves One!

AVNI DIXIT

notionpress.com

INDIA • SINGAPORE • MALAYSIA

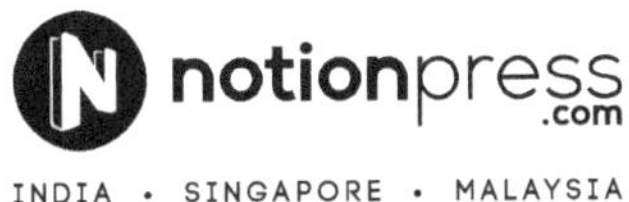

ISBN
Paperback 979-8-89777-886-7
Hardcase 979-8-89984-241-2

Contents

Author's Note

I'm a typical 16-year-old girl who cherishes the little joys in life. Spending time with my friends is always a highlight, and I love playing tennis with my father and younger brother —it's one of those bonding moments that always makes me smile. Mornings, though, are another story. Hitting the snooze button is practically a ritual, and dragging myself out of bed for school feels like climbing a mountain some days. But Saturdays make up for it, especially because they mean our beloved family sushi lunch dates—a tradition I look forward to all week. Debate competitions? Those are my arena. There's something thrilling about standing up in front of an audience, arguing passionately for what I believe in. I also have a deep love for concerts and an adventurous streak that pulls me toward experiences like deep-sea diving, which feels like entering a whole new world.

When it's time to unwind, you'll often find me curled up with a biography or an inspiring story about strong women who've changed the world. Indra Nooyi and Anne Frank are two figures I turn to again and again; their lives and stories guide me, inspire me, and often make for the perfect bedtime read.

Now, let me be honest—I'm not the kind of person who ever thought I would write a book. So, if you've picked this up, be kind with your reading! This is a journey I never expected to take, but one I felt compelled to embark on, and I hope you'll stick with me to the end.

Deep Sea Diving—never afraid to try new things

Like most families in this part of the world, many of my summers have always revolved around our annual trips to India. These vacations are more than just holidays; they're a blend of love, tradition, and connection. We spend time with my paternal grandparents and maternal grandmother, who never fail to shower us with affection and homemade delights. There's laughter, storytelling, and an endless stream of delicious food that seems to taste better simply because it's made by their hands. These trips are also about reconnecting with our extended family, traveling to new places, and embracing the whirlwind of color, culture, and chaos that India offers. But for me, what makes these summers truly special is my time with the girls supported by Gyaanjyoti, a charitable trust devoted to empowering economically underprivileged girls through education.

Doing what I enjoy the most

This ritual has become an essential part of my summers. On each visit, I sit with these girls, talking to them about their dreams, helping them with their studies, and guiding them on possible career paths. There's a bittersweet satisfaction in trying to convince parents to delay or reconsider early marriages for their daughters, reminding them of the power education holds. I've even managed to sponsor a few girls through my pocket money. These small contributions feel like tiny ripples in the vast ocean of change, but they matter. What I love most, though, is sharing stories with them—stories of successes and failures, joys and struggles, silly moments of life, and the serious lessons they teach us. It's in these moments that I feel a deep sense of purpose and connection.

Ons Jabeur: First Arab-North African Woman to Reach a Grand Slam Semi-Final.

This book is born out of those conversations and connections. Through these pages, I hope to share the stories of some truly remarkable girls who have fought against incredible odds to pursue their education. Their courage and determination are nothing short of extraordinary, and I hope their journeys inspire you as much as they've inspired me. Education is not just about learning; it's the key to unlocking a future full of opportunities.

As Malcolm X said -

"Education is the passport to the future, for tomorrow belongs to those who prepare for it today."

So, as you turn these pages, I hope their stories leave a mark on your heart. More importantly, I hope they inspire you to consider how you can make someone's life better—perhaps by supporting their education, mentoring them, or simply believing in their potential. After all, the gift of education is the gift of a brighter tomorrow.

At the final round of World Scholars Cup - Tournament of the Champions at Yale University

A Question That Changed Everything

Sometimes, it takes the smallest gestures to make you question everything you thought you knew. For me, it was one moment—simple, yet unforgettable—that shifted how I saw the world.

When you're sixteen, life often feels like a bubble of school projects, hangouts with friends, and the small dramas of everyday life. You think you know the world because it's the one you see around you every day—familiar, safe, and predictable. But then something happens—a moment, an experience—that bursts that bubble, forcing you to look beyond and see things you never noticed before.

One afternoon two years ago, during my summer break in India, I was in the car, heading back home after my tennis coaching. The car AC hummed softly, cooling the sweat that clung to my skin after practice. My dad, who was in the US at the time, happened to call, and we started chatting about my Tennis session—how my backhand was improving and how my serve had gotten better. Then the conversation shifted to a pair of Nike Jordans that I had been asking him to buy for me.

I could see them vividly in my mind—sleek, stylish, and perfect in every way. They were the kind of shoes that made you feel like you belonged, like you were part of the group. I'd had my eyes on them for a while, and a few of my friends had already snagged them in the trendiest colors. The thought of slipping into those Jordans, of lacing them up before an outing, filled me with a kind of giddy excitement that only a teenager could fully understand. After all, a teenage girl can never have enough shoes, right? As I animatedly talked to my dad about them, I turned my head to glance out of the car window—and that's when I saw them.

A large group of children sat huddled under the sparse shade of a few roadside trees. The trees, though tall, offered little respite from the oppressive August heat, their thin shadows doing little to cool the air, which shimmered with humidity. The kids, of varying ages, sat on rough gunny sacks spread across the cracked, dry ground. For those unfamiliar, gunny sacks are coarse, burlap-like bags used to store grains—hardly the kind of surface anyone would willingly choose to sit on. The sacks were old, fraying at the edges, barely providing a barrier between the children and the unforgiving earth beneath them.

Kids studying in the sweltering heat on a roadside pavement, my first moment of truth

Despite the harsh conditions, the kids were engrossed in what they were doing. Their notebooks were thin and tattered, the pages curling at the edges, held together more by willpower than by their flimsy spines. Yet, they scribbled intently, their heads bent low, their hands moving quickly as if racing against some invisible clock. Some squinted against the harsh sunlight, raising their hands to shield their eyes from the glare as they focused on their studies. Others shifted uncomfortably, tugging at their clothes to adjust to the heat and dust. One boy, no older than ten or twelve, fumbled with his frayed school bag, trying to tie a knot around a tear to keep his belongings from spilling out.

The sight stopped me cold.

The cool air inside the car suddenly felt stifling. My dad's voice faded into the background as I stared at the scene outside. Their focus, their quiet determination, felt like a mirror reflecting something I hadn't let myself see before. I was here, preoccupied with shoes I didn't really need, while they were doing everything they could to learn under conditions that were anything but fair.

For a moment, I felt overwhelmed. Not guilty, but deeply aware. Those kids weren't any less capable or deserving—they simply hadn't been given the same chances. Seeing them made me realize how much of life depends on where you're born, who your parents are, and the resources around you.

It wasn't the first time I had thought about inequality, but it was the first time I felt it so sharply. My bubble of comfort had always felt normal, but now it felt fragile. Privilege didn't feel like something to take for granted anymore—it felt like a responsibility. I started asking myself: What was I doing with all that I had been given?

When I got home that day, I couldn't stop thinking about what I'd seen. The excitement of getting a new pair of Jordans from my dad faded, replaced by thoughts of those kids sitting under the tree. Their faces, their quiet determination, stayed with me. The next day, I found myself drawn back to that spot, wanting to know more. I spoke to the teachers who were helping them, and they told me about the Vikas Vishranti Charitable Trust. It was a place where these kids came to study during the day, and they kindly shared the address with me.

Curiosity led me to visit the trust myself. It wasn't a grand institution—just a modest building with a few rooms and a small courtyard. But the moment I stepped inside, I could feel the vibrant energy and life buzzing through the place. Children of all ages were there, eager to learn. Some were catching up on pending schoolwork, while others were learning practical skills like tailoring, knitting, or crafting—opportunities they wouldn't have found anywhere else.

This wasn't just a place to study; it was a safe haven. For these kids, it represented hope and the possibility of a future beyond what their parents had known. Many lacked access to proper schools or even basic supplies, yet here they found something far more valuable: love, encouragement, and the belief that they could dream of something bigger. It was a place where they could begin to imagine a brighter future—and start working towards making it real.

Mrs. R.K. Usha, the founder and president of the Vikas Vishranthi Charitable Trust, warmly welcomed me. An energetic woman in her 70s, her passion for supporting the marginalized and her belief in the power of ordinary citizens to create positive change led to the establishment of the trust in 2011.

Mrs. Usha gave me a full tour of the vibrant and lively premises. The courtyard was buzzing with activity—older kids were working on computers in the lab, while others were busy at sewing machines, crafting beautiful bags, bedsheets, and tablecloths to showcase and sell at exhibitions.

Later, I did end up buying a lot of items to be gifted to my friends and extended family. Children were creating small handicrafts using recyclable materials, making rakhis as Raksha Bandhan was around the corner, while a few ran around carrying books. Others sat in groups on the floor, diligently writing during their class. In one classroom, an interactive session on a Moral Science topic was underway, with students sincerely sharing their personal stories.

Soon, it was lunchtime. The air was filled with the delicious aroma of home-cooked meals packed by their mothers, blending with cheerful chatter and the clinking of lunchboxes. The energy and purpose in every corner of Vikas Vishranti were truly inspiring.

Among the crowd that day, a little girl stood out. She couldn't stop glancing at me, her shy smile breaking through every few seconds. Once she noticed she had my attention, she carefully made her way toward me, clutching a small steel tiffin in her hands. Her excitement was almost contagious. "You have to taste my mom's cooking—it's so good!" she exclaimed, her voice filled with pride and uncontainable joy. Her eyes sparkled as she began to describe, in vivid detail, how her mom had rolled out the chapatis fresh that very morning and cooked them with love.

At first, I smiled politely and nodded, not fully grasping the weight of the moment. But as I looked closer, I began to understand. Her clothes were slightly worn, her shoes dusty, and her little tiffin wasn't filled with anything gourmet—just chapati and dry vegetable sabzi, a simple yet deeply comforting staple for so many in the Indian diaspora.

In that instant, I realized what she was offering me wasn't just food. This was a piece of her world, a glimpse into her life, something she was fiercely proud to share. Despite having so little, she held that tiffin out to me as if it were the most precious treasure—and in many ways, it was.

I couldn't help but compare this moment with my own privilege. Back at my school, we had a sleek, modern cafeteria with an extensive, almost overwhelming menu. Everything from fresh salads to international dishes, snacks, and desserts was available, all easily accessible and effortlessly affordable for my peers and me.

The thought hit me like a jolt—what a stark contrast. Here was this little girl, offering me what might have been her only meal for the day, beaming with pride and excitement, while I had always taken my endless choices for granted.

Her enthusiasm stayed with me long after that day. It wasn't just her words or actions that struck me; it was the intent behind them. She didn't have much in terms of material things, but she had an abundance of generosity, a raw and unfiltered eagerness to give and share.

It made me stop and question myself: How often do I take the simplest things in life for granted? How often do I let abundance blind me to the beauty of small, heartfelt gestures?

Summer 2023 at Vikas Vishranti NGO: Teaching young minds and learning invaluable lessons from them.

Back home in Dubai, I've never had to worry about having enough of anything. A comfortable home, good food on the table, a great school, regular vacations—these were constants in my life, things I had grown up considering normal. But in that brief interaction, that little girl reminded me of something far more significant: generosity isn't about how much one has. It's about the intent, the genuine desire to share, no matter how small the offering may seem.

That moment taught me a lesson I'll carry with me forever—true giving isn't about the size of the gift but the heart behind it. Her small tiffin, filled with chapati and sabzi, was so much more than just a meal. It was a reflection of pride, love, and an unwavering spirit. It reminded me to pause, appreciate, and never take for granted the privileges I've been blessed with. Most importantly, it showed me that true wealth lies in the willingness to give, even when you have so little to spare.

This brings to mind a quote by Anne Frank, someone I deeply admire. Her diary - ***The Diary of a Young Girl***, has resonated with millions, including me, and one of her lines has always stood out: **"No one has ever become poor by giving."** I remember, during a family vacation to Amsterdam, pestering my parents until they agreed to visit Anne Frank's house on the Prinsengracht Canal. It's now a biographical museum, and walking through her space—seeing where she poured her thoughts into her diary—was a humbling experience that left a lasting impression on me.

Returning to the memory of that little girl and her heartfelt food offering, it stayed with me, not because it made me feel guilty, but because it made me reflect on my responsibility. How could I—someone who has been given so much—do more to support those who haven't been as fortunate?

Until that day, it was not that I was oblivious to the inequalities of the world or the disparities around us. I grew up aware of these issues, thanks to my paternal grandparents' work with GyaanJyoti, a charitable trust they helped co-found to support economically underprivileged girls. I'd watched them tirelessly identify girls in need, arrange sponsorships, and convince families to prioritize education over early marriages. Since I was eleven, I had tagged along, seeing their dedication firsthand and learning what it meant to stand up for others. By the time I turned twelve, I was volunteering myself, helping out however I could. But this moment felt different—it wasn't just something I observed or assisted with from a distance. This time, it felt deeply personal, as if the responsibility was mine to carry forward.

This simple encounter was the beginning of a bigger shift in how I saw my own privilege and the role I could play in someone else's story. As I thought about that girl, her pride in her mom's cooking, and her eagerness to share, one question kept coming back to me: *What more can I do?*

Back in Dubai, life felt almost surreal compared to what I had experienced at Vikas Vishranti. My days were a whirlwind of school assignments and assessments, with most evenings spent practicing on the tennis court as I was also part of my school's Tennis squad or in Debate training as a member of the UAE National debate Development Team. Weekends were a mix of time with family and friends, and life moved along in a steady, predictable rhythm. Everything felt easy—a perfect bubble of convenience and comfort. I never had to think twice about the basics or even the luxuries. There was always enough food, clean water, and an unwavering sense of safety wherever I went. But after my time in India, that seemingly perfect bubble started to feel fragile, as if I could now see the cracks I hadn't noticed before.

The question grew louder in my mind: *What more can I do?* Feeling grateful or blessed wasn't enough. I needed to act, to take some of the privilege I'd been given and turn it into opportunities for someone else. Helping wasn't merely an option—it felt like a responsibility, a way to honor everything I'd been fortunate enough to have.

That thought stayed with me, eventually becoming the thread that connected everything I began to do. My journey of giving had started quite some time before my visit to Vikas Vishranti—through my sponsorship of two economically underprivileged girls, Kajal and Priyanka, via GyaanJyoti, a trust dedicated to empowering young girls by funding their education. They were bright and determined, but their families couldn't afford the education they deserved. Supporting them through my monthly pocket money felt like the right thing to do. Over time, I mentored them from Dubai, celebrated their successes and watched them overcome the challenges they faced.

Each step showed me the transformative power of education. These weren't abstract ideas anymore—they were real girls with real dreams, and education was giving them the tools to pursue them. As rewarding as it was to see Kajal and Priyanka progress through school, the question still lingered: What more can I do?

The answer to that question led me to write this book.

It's more than a collection of stories; it's a way to amplify the voices of girls who deserve to be heard. It reflects my mission to ensure that every girl who wants to get educated has the opportunity to receive one. When you educate a girl, you educate a family, a community and even the nation. I've seen this firsthand through GyaanJyoti. Their journeys filled with resilience, determination and success, show the power of education and the human spirit to overcome challenges.

This book is important to me because of what these stories represent. They show us that change is possible and that small actions can have a ripple effect. Through these narratives, I hope to inspire others to recognize their privilege and ask themselves the same question that changed my life: *What more can I do?*

This book is for anyone who has ever wondered how they can make a difference.

It's for people who, like me, have lived with the comfort of privilege but feel a pull to do more. Maybe you've seen inequality up close—walking through a street, passing by a school, or even hearing someone else's story—or maybe it's something you've read about that lingers in your mind, urging you to think about it more deeply. Either way, this book is here to show you that even the smallest actions can lead to something extraordinary. The smallest step forward can create a ripple that grows into waves of change, touching lives in ways you may never fully realize.

It's also for those who believe in the power of education—not just as a tool for learning, but as a way to transform lives. The stories in this book are proof that change doesn't require grand gestures or massive resources. Sometimes, it's as simple as contributing INR 500 a month for educating a girl or offering support to someone who needs it. These small actions can set off a chain reaction, reaching beyond one individual to uplift families, strengthen communities and inspire generations. Education has the power to rewrite futures, and these stories show how even a single opportunity can unlock potential that would otherwise go unnoticed.

Through these pages, you'll meet girls who faced overwhelming odds and still found ways to overcome them. You'll learn about their dreams, their struggles and their determination to rise above circumstances that could have easily held them back. Their resilience is inspiring, their courage humbling and their achievements a testament to what is possible when someone believes in them. I hope their journeys will make you think about the power we each hold to make a difference—not in some distant or abstract way, but in the everyday choices we make and the opportunities we create for others.

As you read, I hope this leaves you with a sense of hope and possibility.

Change isn't out of reach—it starts with small steps. Steps that anyone can take.

As Martin Luther King Jr. famously said, **"Life's most persistent and urgent question is, 'What are you doing for others?"**

Change begins with looking at the world around us and asking what role we can play in shaping a better future. This book isn't just about their stories—it's about what those stories can inspire in you. It's a reminder that we are all connected and that even the smallest actions can create ripples of hope and change.

Through these stories, I want to show you how small actions can lead to lasting impact. This isn't just about me—it's about all of us and what we can achieve together. If even one reader is inspired to act, to reach out, to make a difference, then this book will have fulfilled its purpose.

CHAPTER 1

Two Worlds, One Truth

I am not Malala. In fact, my childhood could not be more different from hers. I wasn't born in the Swat Valley of Pakistan, where narrow roads wind through the mountains, and diesel fumes linger in the air. I didn't grow up wondering if my walk to school would be interrupted by danger or uncertainty. My world is far removed from that reality. I was born in Dubai, where stepping out of my house each morning means seeing the towering Burj Khalifa glinting in the sunlight. The streets are clean, the roads wide, and everything runs like clockwork. There are no unexpected power cuts and no fear of walking alone in the evening. Safety isn't something I've ever had to question—it has always been a given.

And yet, despite these differences, Malala and I share some things. Like her, I took the bus to school. My previous school was only a ten-minute walk away from home, but I chose the bus not for safety but for the simple joy of those morning moments with my friends. We'd catch up on homework, swap stories, and gossip about the day ahead. It's funny how, no matter where you're from, some things stay the same—girls everywhere find ways to connect over the little things.

We don't choose where we're born, yet it shapes everything: who we are, what we have, and even what we dare to dream. We live in a world where the gap between privilege and struggle often hides in plain sight. It's in the shoes you wear, the roads you walk, the spaces you move through without thinking. Growing up in Dubai, I didn't always notice that gap. On social media and in movies, privilege is easy to spot—it's in the sprawling mansions, the designer bags, the curated vacations, and the "what's in my bag" videos that pop up on every feed. But real privilege? It's quieter. It's the clean streets that you assume will always be there. It's the confidence of stepping out without fear. It's knowing that opportunities are within reach, and that your dreams aren't weighed down by survival.

Privilege, I've come to realize, isn't measured by wealth alone. It's shaped by systems—the ones that decide who gets to thrive and who struggles to get by. In Dubai, those systems work seamlessly. Schools are well-funded. Public spaces are safe. Buses and metros arrive on time, and people follow the rules because they can trust the system to hold up. I never wondered if my school had enough teachers or if the lights would stay on during exams. I never had to think about whether the road to school was safe or if there would even be a school to attend. Things that seemed ordinary to me—catching a metro late at night without worry, walking to a café alone, or leaving my phone on a table and knowing it would still be there when I got back—are luxuries in many parts of the world.

But for a long time, I didn't see it that way. Comfort can make you blind to contrast, especially when you've never had to think about what life might be like without it. Privilege isn't always the loudest thing in the room; sometimes, it's the quiet that surrounds you, the calm you've always known, and opportunities that seem like rights rather than gifts.

And that's where Malala and I part ways again. Her fight was for something I never had to ask for: the right to learn safely, and to dream freely. Mine is about what you do with the comfort you've been given. How do you carry privilege without being consumed by it? How do you use it to make space for someone else? These questions weren't always on my mind. But they are now. And that's where this story really begins.

One of my trips to India when I was 11 was eye-opening in ways I hadn't imagined. It wasn't just a family visit—it was my first experience visiting the NGO GyaanJyoti my grandparents had introduced me to. I remember stepping into a small community center where kids sat cross-legged on the floor, their eyes lighting up as we walked in. They greeted me with wide smiles, some shy, some bold, and eagerly showed me their work—carefully written alphabets, math problems solved on fraying notebooks. It was a world so different from mine, yet their energy and curiosity felt instantly familiar.

As I started to piece these experiences together, I realized how easily I had overlooked the systems that shaped my life. Growing up in Dubai, everything seemed effortless—a privilege born of infrastructure, stability, and years of work that had created a safe and thriving environment. In contrast, the kids I saw at the NGO were growing up in systems that demanded resilience at every turn. It wasn't that they lacked talent or drive; it was that their environment didn't offer the same opportunity for their potential to grow as I had. Many came from broken families, low-income backgrounds, families below the poverty line, or had parents with criminal histories—the list goes on.

Privilege isn't a simple story of "haves" and "have-nots." It's layered and shaped by history, geography, and society. In India, I saw both struggle and strength. Kids like the ones I saw studying on the roadside showed a resilience that seemed unimaginable in my world of convenience. Their perseverance wasn't a heroic narrative—it was a necessity. And yet, their hope felt infectious, their dreams unshaken.

What struck me most wasn't the lack of resources—it was the potential. These kids had the drive to succeed but lacked the tools to do so. The system around them didn't give their dreams the same chance to take flight as mine had. And that's what privilege is: not better talent, not harder work, but a different set of starting conditions. It's the absence of constant barriers.

This realization didn't diminish my gratitude for my life in Dubai—it deepened it. It also forced me to see my role differently. I couldn't change where I was born, and I couldn't change the circumstances of every child I met. But I could use my advantages to create opportunities, to bridge some part of the gap I had started to see more clearly.

Privilege is often invisible until you step outside of it. Once you do, it's impossible to ignore. It's not a bad thing to have—it's what you choose to do with it that matters. That realization grew louder with every trip, every story, and every conversation.

At the time, I didn't have all the answers. I still don't. But I knew I couldn't look away. I started asking myself questions that didn't have easy answers: How do I use what I have to make a difference? What can I do to help bridge the gap between the life I live and the lives I've seen? And, more importantly, how do I do it in a way that honors the strength and dignity of the people who inspired me?

These questions didn't come from guilt—they came from a sense of responsibility. I didn't choose where I was born, but I could choose what I would do with the opportunities I had been given. That's what privilege is: not an endowment but an invitation. An invitation to use what you've been given to help create a world where those invisible barriers start to come down, where more people have the chance to dream freely, to thrive, and to live with the same ease and safety that I had always known.

This realization marked the beginning of a shift in how I saw myself and my role in the world. It was no longer enough to appreciate what I had; I wanted to act on it, to turn gratitude into something tangible. I didn't have a plan yet, but I had a purpose. And it started with acknowledging the privilege I had spent so long taking for granted.

A World of Contrast

Visiting India wasn't stepping into a world of lack; it was stepping into a world of contrasts—a place where vibrancy and challenges coexisted in ways that made me question everything I thought I knew. India wasn't unfamiliar to me; it was where my roots lay, where stories of my family began, and where culture flourished in ways that made every visit memorable. But as I grew older, these visits began to reveal layers I hadn't noticed before.

The first thing that struck me was how alive everything felt. The streets were bursting with life—rickshaws zigzagging through traffic, vendors calling out to passersby, and kids chasing after makeshift cricket balls in narrow lanes. I remember one of our visits when my mother insisted on taking us on an auto-rickshaw ride. For her, it was nostalgic; for us, it was an adventure. She regaled us with stories of her childhood—riding rickshaws for outings with friends or eating paani puri from street vendors, which left me and my brother both aghast and amused. My younger brother clung to me nervously as the auto bounced over potholes, his underweight frame nearly flying out, an incredulous look of dismay on his face as we hit a particularly deep one. It was chaotic and thrilling, a moment that stayed with me for its humor and how vividly it highlighted the differences in our everyday realities. Every corner seemed to have its own pulse and with it, a sense of community that felt both chaotic and comforting.

Yet, India's contrasts aren't confined to bustling city streets or quiet village lanes—they stretch across regions, cities, and neighborhoods. My trips to the National Capital Region

(NCR) made this even clearer. Delhi's historic charm stands alongside the modern skyline of Gurgaon, where glass-fronted office buildings, luxury malls, and rooftop cafes cater to a fast-paced urban lifestyle. Gurgaon pulses with corporate energy, tech parks, and an ever-expanding metro network. Drive some 50-odd kilometers, and you find yourself in Noida, where residential high-rises overlook sprawling malls and tech hubs. Greater Noida, where my grandparents live, is yet another world altogether—green, spacious, and planned. Wide roads lined with trees guide you past residential sectors, prestigious colleges, and emerging landmarks. The city boasts the massive Jaypee Sports Complex, home to an international racing circuit and myriad facilities that host everything from tennis tournaments to motorsport events. There's also the under-construction international airport, promising to transform connectivity and development further. It's remarkable how one area holds such a high concentration of universities and colleges, reflecting India's drive toward education and growth. Development here isn't subtle—it's loud, fast, and ever-evolving. Yet, amid the towering buildings and modern infrastructure, you still spot roadside tea stalls, street vendors, and children playing outside their homes, underscoring the everyday dualities that define India.

Amid this energy, there were moments that stopped me in my tracks—moments that made me notice the gaps. The gaps weren't just individual—they were systemic. According to UDISEPlus 2023–24 data, approximately 47.44 million children aged 6 to 17 years are out of school in India, representing about 16.8% of the total child population in this age group. For many, the barriers weren't just about attending school but overcoming challenges like malnutrition. According to the 2024 GHI report, India ranks 105th out of 127 countries, classified under the 'serious' category. This raises questions about food security in India, especially for a country that is often hailed as a rapidly growing economy. The report states that India's malnutrition level is 'serious.' In India, child stunting (35.5%) and wasting (19.7%) are at concerning levels. Stunting refers to low height for age, and wasting refers to low weight for height—both of which has a detrimental effect on a child's overall development, leaving them stunted and struggling to learn effectively. Standing in the midst of Greater Noida's wide avenues, surrounded by new developments, it was hard to reconcile how pockets of abundance and deprivation could sit so close to each other. While some children head to well-equipped international schools, others in the same city face classrooms without proper desks, outdated textbooks, and no reliable electricity. It's these contrasts—sometimes a matter of just a few kilometers—that reveal the complex layers of India. It's vibrant and resilient, yes, but also a place where privilege and struggle often share the same view.

These visits to India, with all their colors, sounds, and complexities, stayed with me. They taught me that privilege isn't always about grand displays of wealth—it's sometimes in the unnoticed things: the clean roads, healthy food, uninterrupted power, and safe routes to school. India, with all its contrasts, didn't just show me differences—it made me reflect on what I've always taken for granted.

It wasn't that every child in India faced these circumstances. That would be an oversimplification of a country as vast and diverse as India. For every child studying under a banyan tree, struggling with limited resources, there are countless stories of Indians who have risen to global prominence. India is home to some of the brightest minds, with leaders like Sundar Pichai, Satya Nadella, and Indra Nooyi helming Fortune 500 companies in the US. This stark contrast highlights the dual reality of the nation—on one hand, children grappling with systemic inadequacies, and on the other, individuals who've broken barriers to achieve extraordinary success.

India also leads in industries like technology, space exploration, and education, driven by communities and organizations working tirelessly to bridge these gaps. Yet, the disparities remain undeniable. This duality made me reflect on the systems that shaped my life. What created the difference between the opportunities I had in Dubai and the challenges some kids faced here? It wasn't about individual effort—it was about access. It was about how the systems around us either opened doors or kept them firmly shut.

At the same time, what stood out to me wasn't just the challenges—it was the strength and ingenuity I saw everywhere. There were kids who found ways to study despite the odds, families who worked together to create better futures, and communities that celebrated small victories, whether it was a child passing an exam or a street lit up for a festival. It reminded me that privilege isn't just about resources—it's about having the freedom to dream without barriers. And that freedom wasn't equally distributed.

These visits didn't leave me feeling guilty or overwhelmed, they left me inspired. Inspired by the hope I saw in the eyes of kids who believed in something better, even when the odds seemed stacked against them. I was inspired by the hope I saw in the eyes of kids who believed in something better, even when the odds seemed stacked against them, and by the parents and teachers who worked tirelessly to create opportunities where there seemed to be none. I was inspired to think about my own life and my newfound purpose, which is to help make the gap a little smaller.

Realizing Inequality

It was during one of those visits to a village in Haryana with my grandparents, to canvass for girl education that I met her in the summer of 2023—a girl my age, living a life so different from mine that it felt like we were on opposite ends of the world. We were in a small village, surrounded by fields that stretched as far as the eye could see. The air smelled of earth, and the hum of daily life moved at a pace far slower than the lively cities I was used to.

She greeted me shyly, her hands clutching the edge of her dupatta. Her name was Anjali, and she was fourteen, just like me then. But that's where the similarities ended. While I was juggling school projects and planning my next outing with friends, she was helping her family make ends meet. She had dropped out of school two years earlier to care for her younger siblings and help her mother in the fields.

Her story mirrored that of many girls in rural India, where 40% of girls aged 15-18 drop out of school, often due to family responsibilities or early marriage. Globally, 129 million girls are out of school, their education disrupted by systemic barriers that go far beyond individual circumstances.

Her eyes lit up when she spoke about the subjects she had loved in school, especially science. "I wanted to be a teacher," she said, almost in a whisper, as if the dream still lingered somewhere deep inside her. But that dream had been put on hold, maybe indefinitely. The weight of her responsibilities was too heavy, and there was no system in place to ease the burden.

That conversation stayed with me long after we said goodbye. It was more than just her story—it was the realization that our lives had been shaped by forces far beyond our control. Anjali was no less intelligent or less ambitious than I was. She simply didn't have the same opportunities. Her world demanded sacrifices that mine never had.

That night, as I sat at the desk in my grandparents' house in India, surrounded by stacks of books and the soft hum of the ceiling fan, her face lingered in my thoughts, returning to me again and again. I turned on the desk lamp, and the light felt jarring. It reminded me of the hours she spent studying by the dim glow of a single bulb or sometimes a flickering candle. Every little thing around me—electricity, clean water, even the chair I sat on—felt like a gift I had never fully acknowledged.

This wasn't about comparing lives or feeling sorry for someone else; it was about understanding how differently life unfolds depending on the circumstances one is born into. It's the freedom to pursue dreams without the constant weight of survival. That moment with Anjali wasn't the first time I had thought about inequality, but it was the first time it felt personal—not an abstract idea or something I read about, but something real, staring back at me and making me question everything I thought I understood about fairness and opportunity. I realized then that the systems that had effortlessly supported me could also be leveraged to change lives for others. Anjali didn't need pity; she needed a path forward, the kind of support that would let her dream again. And while I couldn't change everything, I could start somewhere. The thought of her teaching a classroom full of eager students stayed with me, a reminder of the power of potential and how easily it could be lost without the right support.

That's when I began to see my own role differently. Finding ways to contribute, to make even the smallest difference, ensured that stories like hers didn't have to stay unfinished. That realization became real for me; I had witnessed it firsthand in the lives of those closest to me, and it strengthened my resolve to keep moving forward.

The Role of Resilience

Some of the most important lessons I've learned about resilience came not from strangers but from the people closest to me—my grandparents. For as long as I can remember, their lives have revolved around education, not just for their own children but for anyone who needed it. Their home has always been a space filled with the hum of young voices, the scratching of pencils, and the quiet determination of students eager to learn.

Every evening at 5 p.m., eight to ten children would arrive at their doorstep. My grandparents would greet them warmly, inviting them in for an hour or two of lessons in math and English. These weren't children from affluent families. Many of them walked long distances to reach their home, their notebooks tucked under their arms, their faces lit with hope. They often came from neighboring villages, some leaving home much earlier just to arrive before time to play in the courtyard before lessons began. Rain or shine, they rarely missed a class. Even during heavy rains, when asked why they hadn't just stayed home, they would reply with bright smiles, saying they loved being there.

The lessons extended beyond academics. My grandparents didn't just teach math and english—they taught them to dream, to believe that education could change their lives. On special occasions like Republic Day and national holidays, they would take the children on picnics, giving them a rare chance to enjoy and explore beyond their usual routines. Once in a while, they would organize dance sessions at home. The living room would fill with laughter, music, and the smell of light snacks being served. Moments like these made their home more than just a place to study—it was a haven where the children felt safe and empowered.

In class, the energy was palpable. The children were eager to answer questions, to come up to the board and write, and to cheer each other on. They found joy in learning and encouraged one another, creating an environment of mutual support and motivation. I also taught a few classes during my stay there.It was truly inspiring to see their determination and enthusiasm.

Enjoyed teaching the kids in the evenings during my summer vacation of 2024

Their work felt even more significant in a world where 10.1 million child laborers in India aged 5 to 14 are deprived of basic rights like education. For these children, the chance to learn is not an opportunity—it's a rare lifeline. And my grandparents, through their tireless efforts, gave them not only education but a sense of hope, joy, and belonging.

Education has always been at the heart of my family's story. In 1968, my grandfather graduated from IIT Kanpur with a degree in mechanical engineering and encouraged my dadi (grandmother) to pursue her PhD in history after they got married—a rare and progressive choice for their time. Together, they would embark on a two-and-a-half-hour journey from Nangal to Chandigarh on their Lambretta scooter. My grandmother would sit behind my grandfather while their two young kids, aged 2 and 5, were sandwiched between them. My father often jokes about spending his early childhood clinging to my Dadi's dupatta like a lifeline, desperately trying not to fall off the scooter while dodging the flying dust of rural Punjab's roads. It was chaotic, endearing, and a perfect reflection of their unwavering determination to prioritize education against all odds.

That belief ran even deeper, passed down through generations. My Dada's mother, my great-grandmother, pursued an education at a time when it was unheard of for women, especially after marriage, to do so. She became a principal, supported by her husband, my great-grandfather, who was a practicing lawyer. In the 1930s, during pre-independent India, this was a bold and unconventional path. She would leave her home on a bicycle to attend college but only ride it after she was outside the premises of her conservative community, where such actions were frowned upon. She didn't let societal norms dictate her choices, setting an example that would ripple across generations.

This legacy of perseverance and belief in education profoundly shaped my grandparents' lives and work. Together, they co-founded GyaanJyoti with like-minded people, a charitable trust dedicated to empowering underprivileged girls through education. My Dada, a retired Chief General Manager from National Fertilizers Ltd., serves as the Managing Trustee of GyaanJyoti, continuing his journey of service even after decades in a leadership role. My Dadi, a retired Girl's college Principal, approached every challenge with patience and purpose, mentoring young girls and encouraging families to send their daughters to school.

What stood out to me was not only their actions but the way they found fulfillment in those actions. Their joy came from the small victories—watching a student pass an exam, hearing about a scholarship awarded, or knowing that one more child could stay in school because of their efforts. They weren't trying to change the world overnight. They did what they could, one child at a time, and it created ripples of change. They talked about their enriching experience and encouraged their friends to join GyaanJyoti or volunteer.

It wasn't only the children they helped—it was the perspective they brought to every interaction. Even in the simplest moments, like talking to a taxi driver about his kids or asking the street vendors about their families, they showed genuine care and interest. This deep-rooted belief in the power of education wasn't limited to my paternal grandparents.

My maternal grandmother's journey was equally inspiring. Despite facing fierce opposition from her father, she pursued her studies and completed her graduation, encouraged all the way by her own mother, who was illiterate but believed in the value of education. That education became her lifeline when tragedy struck—widowed at just 24 with two young children (my mother was four, and my uncle was one), she chose not to remarry and instead focused on raising her children independently by starting to work. In the 1970s, that wasn't an easy choice. Yet, her determination and the empowerment that came from her education helped her build a life for her family against the odds.

Both my grandmothers became powerful role models in my life, showing me that resilience isn't just about surviving hardships but about finding purpose in them. They taught me to face challenges head-on and choose to act, even when the path isn't clear. Their lives showed me that fulfillment comes not from what you accumulate but from the lives you touch. Their work taught me that success isn't personal—it's collective.

These lessons stayed with me as I reflected on the lives of the kids I had met during my visits to India. Their resilience wasn't only admirable—it was transformative. It made me rethink what it means to be strong, to be hopeful, and to find meaning in the face of adversity. Watching them, I realized that strength isn't having it easy; it's pushing forward, no matter how hard the journey gets.

My grandparents' unwavering belief in the power of education—and the resilience I saw in those kids—shaped the way I began to see my own life. I didn't have all the answers, but I knew I wanted to carry their mission forward in my own way. If they could devote their lives to creating change, then surely I could find a way to make a meaningful impact as well.

Where Dreams Begin

We don't choose where we're born, yet it shapes everything: who we are, what we have, and even what we dare to dream. But what I've come to understand is that this doesn't have to be the end of the story. Where we start doesn't have to dictate where we end up—not for us and not for others.

The opportunities I've had, the people I've met, and the lessons I've learned have taught me that the advantages we've been given can be amplified to create a broader impact.

During the COVID-19 pandemic, as education shifted online, only 15% of rural households in India had internet access. This stark digital divide highlighted the urgent need to create opportunities that go beyond geography and privilege, ensuring that access to education isn't left to chance.

I vividly remember my Dada calling me often during that time, asking if we had any spare phones or devices to send to kids in India so they could keep studying. It was a simple yet powerful reminder that even the smallest act can make a meaningful difference in someone's education.

But providing phones and laptops was just the beginning.

I found myself roped into a whole new adventure: helping kids actually figure out how to use them. Every weekend, I'd hop onto a Zoom session to give demo lessons—everything from "Here's how you unmute yourself" (a lesson some adults still need!) to teaching kids how to navigate their online classes. There was this one boy, Raj, who was an absolute genius at math—he could solve problems faster than I could google the answers. Teaching him meant I had to brush up on my mathematics skills as if life depended on it. Let's just say he kept me on my toes, and I may or may not have recruited a calculator as my secret weapon.

Then there were the younger kids. Teaching basic English through phonics was an adventure in itself. I had completely forgotten how tricky it was to explain why "k" was silent in the word "knife" and why "No" and "Know" sound the same but have such different meanings—English is truly wild when you think about it! The kids were wonderfully curious, but keeping them engaged online was a different ballgame. My rudimentary Hindi, combined with their non-existent English, made for some interesting exchanges. Once, a little girl, Priya, tried to teach me the Hindi word for "hippopotamus" (which I'm still not sure I've mastered), and in return, I introduced her to "supercalifragilisticexpialidocious." Not exactly balanced, but we had a good laugh.

And then there was the challenge of keeping them from getting distracted. I mean, who could blame them? If I were 8 years old with a laptop in front of me, I'd probably want to explore every corner of YouTube instead of learning multiplication tables. One time, midway through a session, I noticed a boy giggling suspiciously. Turns out, he had found a way to turn himself into a potato filter on Zoom and was absolutely delighted with his new look.

I couldn't even be mad—it was just too funny. There was something so pure about watching someone's childhood unfold right in front of you like that. The sheer joy, the unfiltered curiosity, the excitement of discovering something as simple and silly as a Zoom filter—it was infectious. For a moment, it was like you could see the world through their eyes, where even the smallest things could spark wonder. But then it hit me—a moment like that, as trivial as it might seem, is also a privilege. Not every kid gets the chance to experience that kind of carefree joy, and realizing that made the moment feel both heartwarming and bittersweet.

These moments were exhausting, chaotic, and, honestly, some of the most rewarding work I've ever done. What started as a task to help kids stay connected to their classes became a lesson for me in patience, creativity, and the joy of small victories. Behind every session, there was a sense of hope— that even in the middle of a crisis, we could find ways to help each other rise.

A good education, a safe community, or even a single act of kindness can ripple out in ways we can't always see, creating space for others to hope and dream beyond the limits of their circumstances. For a long time, I thought the only thing that separated me from the kids I met during my visits to India was luck. But now I see it's bigger than that. It's systems, choices, and a shared responsibility to bridge the gaps that divide us.

This book is my humble effort. It's a way to share the stories that have stayed with me, the lessons I've learned, and the hope I've found in unexpected places. It's an invitation— to myself and anyone reading this—to think about how we can use what we have to help others build what they deserve. And if that involves becoming a part-time phonics teacher or a potato filter enthusiast along the way, so be it!

Because, at the heart of it, I believe this: we all have the ability to create change. It might not feel like much at first, but every step forward—every conversation, every opportunity offered—has the power to make a difference. It's not about fixing everything all at once. It's about starting somewhere, anywhere, and knowing that even the smallest ripple can become a wave. As the famous saying goes: **"There is nothing permanent except change."**

Change is inevitable, but how we shape it is up to us. This is the message I hope will carry through the pages of this book. It's not a call for pity or guilt–it's a call to action. A call to see the world not as it is, but as it could be and to take even the smallest steps to make that vision a reality.

We don't choose where we're born, but we can choose what we do with the lives we're given. And when we choose to create opportunities for others, we don't just help them break free from their limitations—we free ourselves from ours, too. Together, we can build a world where dreams aren't dictated by where you come from, but by where you want to go.

"Start where you are.
Use what you have.
Do what you can."

– Arthur Ashe

CHAPTER 2

Faces of Hope, Stories of Strength

In India, nearly 40% of girls aged 15 to 18 are not attending school. This issue extends beyond national borders; globally, approximately 119 million girls are out of school, with 58 million being of upper-secondary school age.

You've probably heard statistics like this before—I know I have. Numbers flash across news screens or pop up in school presentations. They're the kind of facts we register for a second, maybe nod along to, and then move on with our day. They're everywhere, and after a while, they almost stop feeling real.

But every number represents a person. Each percentage point is someone with a story—a life filled with dreams, struggles, and moments of hope. When you stop and think about it, it's overwhelming. How many of these stories go unnoticed? How many dreams end before they even begin?

While systemic barriers often feel abstract, their true weight becomes clear when tied to real lives. These barriers aren't just about finances—they're woven into gender norms, societal expectations, and gaps in infrastructure that make even basic education a battle for many.

For me, this particular statistic became personal when I met Sakshi and Varsha—two girls whose stories turned these numbers into something real. Until then, disparities in education were something I understood in theory. Meeting them changed that.

Their names were among the first I heard during my time with GyaanJyoti dedicated to supporting underprivileged children's education. I still remember the day vividly—the quiet murmur of conversations, the warm welcome from the team, and then the moment when two pairs of eyes filled with determination caught my attention.

They were sisters who grew up in Panipat, a city in India known for its textile industry but also shaped by significant economic challenges. Their family lived simply, relying on their father's small shop, which often struggled because of his chronic health problems. While the city seemed lively, opportunities for girls like Sakshi and Varsha were few, making progress a constant challenge.

Sakshi and Varsha weren't just a statistical number; they were sisters with dreams that felt impossibly big for the small city they came from.

Sakshi was the older of the two. Her quick smile and the energy she brought into the room made her stand out. She tied her hair back in a no-nonsense ponytail, her salwar kameez faintly stained from her morning hockey practice. Yes, hockey. Sakshi wasn't just a girl from a small town; she was a national hockey player. She balanced rigorous training with academic pressures that would overwhelm most of us. But it wasn't her athletic achievements that struck me—it was her unwavering focus. She spoke about her dream of becoming a police officer with a conviction that felt like a promise.

Her potential didn't go unnoticed. A generous sponsor from Australia, deeply impressed by her determination and achievements, stepped in to support her education. This sponsorship not only eased some of the financial burden on her family but also became a source of motivation for Sakshi, reinforcing her belief that her dreams were worth pursuing.

Then there was Varsha, quieter but equally determined and also playing hockey at the national level. She joined GyaanJyoti at just eight years old, wide-eyed and brimming with curiosity. She still recalls the thrill of clearing her first scholarship. She carried an oversized school bag that seemed almost too big for her, but the curiosity in her eyes revealed a love for learning that was anything but small. "It felt like someone saw me," she said once, describing what that scholarship meant to her. It wasn't just financial support—it was validation. A reminder that her potential was real, and her dreams mattered.

Varsha—supported by GyaanJyoti, dreaming big. Hockey is her passion.

But behind that determination lay daily struggles that many overlook. Their father runs a small shop that brings in a modest income, and their mother, Sunita, works tirelessly to support the family—teaching during the day and sewing clothes in the evenings to help cover expenses. Her resilience shaped her daughters' outlook on life. "Education is the only thing no one can take away from you," she often reminded them. Those words weren't just advice; they became the foundation of every choice Varsha and Sakshi made.

Their lives were full of sacrifices, often shaped by societal expectations as much as financial limitations. Sakshi, now 21, has completed her NCC (National Cadet Corps) and graduated in Economics & Maths. She has started her Masters program and is now preparing for her sub-inspector exam in July 2025. Yet, even as she works toward her dreams, she faces constant pressure from relatives who insist she should be married by now. Some criticize her for prioritizing education over marriage, pointing out how her height—5'8"—makes finding a "suitable match" harder. These comments reflect the deeply ingrained beliefs that boys education and government jobs are worth investing in, while girls should settle into domestic roles.

Varsha, now 18, is in her second year of a Bachelor of Computer Applications program with an impressive 9.45 CGPA. She is also preparing for NIT (National Institute of Technology) along with her graduation. Her scholarship has been a lifeline, lifting some of the financial strain from her family's shoulders. With exams starting soon, her days are a whirlwind of studying, chores and navigating the challenges of being a young woman pursuing education in an environment where not everyone understands her ambition. Morning hockey practice, a source of both discipline and joy, comes with its risks—she often carries her hockey stick not just for the game but for her safety, wary of the inappropriate comments she hears when returning home late. Despite these hurdles, she presses on, focused on the future she's determined to build.

Their challenges go beyond money and studies. Sakshi has skipped school trips to avoid adding to her family's expenses, while Varsha grapples with the societal pressure of seeing peers—including a cousin married at 19—settle into roles she's not yet ready to assume. In their community, early marriage is common, with some girls married off as young as 13. But with the unwavering support of their parents, Sakshi and Varsha have pushed back against these expectations, carving out their own path.

What's remarkable is how their determination has not only fueled their own journeys but inspired those around them. Their family extends its values beyond their household—teaching local girls sewing skills to promote financial independence and offering others the same encouragement and tools that have helped Sakshi and Varsha chase their dreams.

On countless scorching afternoons, Sakshi would return from hockey practice, her stick slung over her shoulder. The sweat and grit on her face told the story of hours of intense training. Nearby, Varsha would sit deeply focused on sketching a circuit diagram, fully absorbed in solving a complex problem. Watching them side by side, it was clear they were more than just two girls tackling life's challenges—they were breaking barriers, defying expectations, and carving their own path to greatness. In these seemingly ordinary moments, their extraordinary determination and drive stood out.

It was at that moment I came to a deeper realization: Education isn't just about helping individuals move forward—it's about creating ripples of change that uplift entire communities. Their determination showed me that investing in education doesn't just shape lives; it builds a foundation for a brighter, more empowered future.

Education has the power to change lives. According to UNESCO, every additional year of schooling for a girl can increase her future earnings by up to 20% and reduce the likelihood of early marriage by 10%. These aren't just numbers—they're proof of what's possible when barriers are removed and opportunities are created.

Numbers tell us what's happening, but stories like Sakshi and Varsha show why it matters, plus when we put names and faces to numbers.

Systemic Barriers and Resilience

The challenges Sakshi and Varsha faced weren't unique to them. Their story mirrors the struggles of countless girls across India, where education often feels more like a privilege than a basic right. This mindset builds invisible walls that are almost impossible to climb without extraordinary determination.

In their community, educating girls was still considered optional—a luxury rather than a necessity. Marriage and domestic responsibilities took precedence for most families, setting off a cycle that kept girls from dreaming beyond these roles. But it wasn't just about attitudes—it was how these beliefs shaped everyday realities. Schools were overcrowded, textbooks outdated, and opportunities scarce, making ambition feel like an indulgence rather than a possibility.

These barriers—financial strain, societal norms, and infrastructure gaps—are all interconnected. According to UNICEF, girls in rural areas are 20% less likely to complete secondary education compared to boys. And the consequences go far beyond school. A lack of education limits their ability to make independent decisions, earn a stable income, or secure a better future.

For Sakshi, these challenges became most visible when she had to give up hockey—a sport where she had earned national level recognition. Her decision wasn't about passion or talent; it was about survival. With limited local programs and financial pressures mounting as she pursued higher education, continuing the sport became impossible. Letting go of her dream was painful, but she carried the lessons from the field—discipline, resilience, and determination—into her academic journey, setting her sights on becoming a police officer to challenge the very systems that had failed her.

Varsha's obstacles looked different but were no less daunting. Fascinated by technology, she pursued coding despite limited access to devices or resources. Her journey required relentless improvisation—borrowing books, jotting down code by hand, and seizing every learning opportunity she could find. Her quiet persistence paid off when she enrolled in a BCA program, proving that determination can flourish even in the harshest environments.

What makes their story powerful isn't just their success—it's how they transformed obstacles into fuel. Systemic barriers can seem abstract, but they manifest in everyday choices: like skipping a school trip to save money, studying after a day filled with chores, or navigating streets where girls often face harassment. Overcoming these hurdles required more than personal grit—it demanded community support, better schools, and a shift in values.

It's easy to feel overwhelmed by statistics—like 40% of girls dropping out of school.

But numbers alone can't capture the quiet moments of persistence—the late-night studying after an exhausting day or the early mornings spent chasing a dream that others say isn't worth pursuing. For Sakshi and Varsha, those small, deliberate acts added up, shaping not just their journey but the possibilities for girls like them everywhere.

Moments of Transformation

If there's one thing these girls taught me, it's that transformation doesn't always come with a round of applause.

Often, it's in the quiet, persistent choices people make every day—decisions that may seem small but require immense courage. For Sakshi and Varsha, change wasn't sparked by a single moment. It was built step by step, through deliberate actions taken despite challenges that could have easily stopped them.

When I first met them through GyaanJyoti, I was young and didn't immediately grasp the depth of their resilience. They seemed like any other young women—polite and unassuming. But as their stories unfolded, it became clear how extraordinary their journey was. Their determination wasn't loud; it was steady, like a current beneath the surface—strong enough to carry them through trials many would find overwhelming.

Their challenges didn't define them—their response did. Sakshi's path shifted when she had to let go of her hockey dreams. It wasn't a decision she took lightly. She had excelled at the sport, finding purpose and strength on the field. However, financial pressures and the lack of local programs forced her to redirect her focus. What could have been a loss became fuel for something bigger: her goal of becoming a police officer. For her, it was more than a career—it was a chance to challenge the barriers that had stood in her way.

Varsha's transformation took shape in quieter ways. Her fascination with technology, nurtured through borrowed books and makeshift study sessions, was rooted in a belief that her curiosity deserved space to grow. Her scholarship wasn't just financial relief—it was recognition. That validation became a turning point, pushing her to pursue her BCA studies with determination, even when access to basic resources remained limited.

What stood out wasn't just their persistence—it was how their personal victories ignited hope in others. At a local GyaanJyoti event, younger girls listened to their stories. "If they can do it, why can't we?" one asked. That shift—from doubt to possibility—was perhaps the most powerful change of all. Transformation isn't just about personal success; it ripples outward, challenging norms and inspiring others to dream beyond what they thought possible.

Remember that statistic I mentioned earlier? UNESCO reports that every additional year of schooling for a girl can increase her future earnings by up to 20% and lower her chances of early marriage by 10%. Sakshi and Varsha are living proof of what those numbers mean when they translate into real life impact. They didn't just beat the odds—they're changing what's possible for girls in their community.

Their journey shows that transformation isn't always dramatic.

It lives in small victories—the decision to shift focus, the courage to keep going despite setbacks, and the quiet belief that tomorrow can be better. When resilience meets opportunity, extraordinary things happen.

Date..................

मैं वर्षा मिश्रा, BCA II year student. मुझे class 4th से ज्ञानज्योति scholarship मिल रही है। मैं हॉकी की National player हूँ। ज्ञानज्योति scholarship से मुझे बहुत help मिली है। ज्ञानज्योति परिवार से मुझे सिर्फ financial ही नहीं बल्कि Guidence और inspiration भी मिलती है। मैं Graduation के साथ-साथ NIT की तैयारी कर रही हूँ। ज्ञानज्योति scholarship से सपनों को उड़ान मिल गयी है। BCA (Bachelor of Computer Application), करने का सपना, पूरा न हो पाता लेकिन जबसे ज्ञानज्योति परिवार से जुड़ी हूँ मेरे सपनों को जैसे नयी उड़ान मिल गयी है। अभी मैं II year में हूँ, 1st year मैंने 9.54 SGPA score की है। class 12th में भी 92% score किया था। अगर मैं ज्ञानज्योति परिवार से न जुड़ी होती तो शायद आज यहाँ तक न पहुँच पाती, मेरी जैसी न जाने कितनी लड़कियों की life को नयी राह मिली है। मैं हमेशा इस support के लिये grateful रहूँगी और successful होने के बाद मैं भी दो girls को scholarship दुंगी। जो help मुझे मिली है वही help मैं भी करूंगी।

वर्षा मिश्रा

Teacher's Sign ....

GyaanJyoti helped Varsha pursue her dreams, while many other girls in her village couldn't even go to school.

Date....................

मैं साक्षी मिश्रा, M.A Final year की student हूँ। मैं वर्ष 2015 से ज्ञानज्योति scholar हूँ। ज्ञानज्योति scholarship से मुझे मेरी पढ़ाई में बहुत help मिली है। मैं NCC (National Cadet Corps) 'C' certificate holder हूँ। ज्ञानज्योति ट्रस्ट हमें हमेशा motivate and inspire करता है। ज्ञानज्योति ट्रस्ट से मेरी life को अच्छी direction मिली। ज्ञानज्योति ट्रस्ट ने मेरे साथ-साथ बहुत लड़कियों की life को नयी दिशा दी है। जिस जगह से मैं हूँ, वहाँ girls पढ़ना आसान नही हैं, वहाँ से मैं आज M.A कर पा रही हूँ, इसमें ज्ञानज्योति का बहुत बड़ा योगदान है। ज्ञानज्योति ट्रस्ट हम girls के सपनों को नयी उड़ान दे रहा है। ज्ञानज्योति की financial help से मेरे academics को बहुत support मिला। मैं मेरे career के लक्ष्य को पाने के एक कदम और करीब पहुँच रही हूँ। ज्ञानज्योति scholarship से inspire होकर मैंने निर्णय किया है, कि मैं भी सफल होने के बाद एक लड़की की ऐसे ही help करूँगी। जिस प्रकार ज्ञानज्योति scholarship से मेरे सपनो को उड़ान मिली मैं भी किसी के सपनो को उड़ान देना चाहूँगी।

साक्षी मिश्रा

Sakshi's testimonial on how GyaanJyoti supported and motivated her for higher studies.

Small Steps, Big Changes

Stories like Sakshi and Varsha's make you pause. They're not the kind you hear and forget—they linger, reshaping how you see the world. Meeting them made me wonder: How often do we truly notice the struggles around us? Inequality and barriers aren't new topics—we hear about them on the news, in classrooms, or in casual conversations—but how often do we stop to think about the real lives behind those statistics?

It's easy to get lost in routine. Think about the last time you passed a school. Did you notice the children playing in the yard? Did you wonder if they all had the same chance to succeed? For many kids, education isn't a given—it's something they fight for every day. I saw that fight firsthand in Sakshi and Varsha's journey, but theirs wasn't the only story that stayed with me.

There was also Geeta. A girl whose energy was contagious—she loved to dance, to run relays, her feet quick and her spirit even quicker. But no matter how fast she ran, she couldn't outrun the harsh realities that awaited her. At thirteen, while I spent nights strategizing for debate competitions and worrying about school deadlines, Geeta was grappling with decisions no child should face. Her family, weighed down by financial strain, married her off after the eighth grade—no dowry, no choice, just the pressure of tradition and survival.

Her world shifted from classrooms and playgrounds to household chores and whispered conversations that didn't include her. Then, one day, she overheard something that turned her blood cold—a conversation between her husband and mother-in-law plotting to burn her alive as punishment for the dowry she never brought. It was terrifying, yet it was the memory of something seemingly small that saved her: her education. She remembered the letters she once scribbled in school, the words that, until then, felt like lessons on a page.

With trembling hands, she wrote to her parents. That letter—just ink on paper—became her lifeline. Her family received it in time. They came for her, pulling her back from the brink of a future she hadn't chosen.

Geeta's story is a reminder that education isn't just about books or grades—it's about power. It's about having a voice when the world tries to silence you. Her ability to write that letter wasn't luck; it was the direct result of a chance she'd once been given—the chance to learn.

What moved me most about all three girls wasn't just their struggles but how they refused to be defined by them. Sakshi let go of her hockey dreams but found a new purpose in becoming a police officer. Varsha's fascination with technology pushed her to keep learning despite endless obstacles. And Geeta? She used knowledge to fight for her life—literally. Different paths, different challenges, but the same unwavering belief: things could be better.

Their stories also made me reflect on our role in this larger picture. Systemic changes are vital, but small, intentional actions matter just as much. One scholarship changed Sakshi and Varsha's future. One teacher's encouragement planted the seed of possibility. One letter saved Geeta's life. What if more people stepped up? What if we noticed those struggling to rise and chose to offer help—be it through a donation, a conversation, or simply by acknowledging their effort?

Change doesn't always come from monumental efforts. Sometimes, it's the quiet decisions that spark ripples far beyond what we expect. A book given, a hand extended, a word of encouragement—these moments don't make headlines, but they change lives.

So, when was the last time you noticed someone striving to overcome their circumstances? A child eager to learn, a friend balancing work and study, a neighbor chasing a dream against all odds? What did you do in that moment? Because each of us holds the power to create those quiet turning points for someone else.

Sakshi, Varsha, and Geeta rose above challenges that could have easily consumed them. Imagine what's possible if more of us choose to notice, to care, to act. Changing one life doesn't stop there—it touches families, strengthens communities, and inspires the world.

I've seen it happen. And now, you have too.

This is the kind of world we can build—one small, meaningful step at a time. A world where kindness isn't just a thought but an action. A world where lifting one person creates waves far beyond ourselves.

I want to be part of that world—don't you?

As Malala once said, **"One book, one pen, one child, and one teacher can change the world."**

It all starts with a small step toward making a difference.

CHAPTER 3

A Mission in Motion

Education is the most powerful weapon that you use to change the world - Nelson Mandela

For as long as I can remember, education has been at the center—if not the thread running through—every part of my life.

And the way to get there? It starts with school.

From early mornings spent rushing to finish assignments to late nights cramming formulas, from meeting friends to loving some subjects and not quite enjoying others, school wasn't just a place of learning—it felt like a second home, with 7 to 8 hours of my day spent there. Over the years, I attended quite a few schools, transitioning from the British curriculum to the Indian system before finally settling into an IB school. As the eldest child, my parents carefully considered every school choice and its impact, ensuring the best fit for me. Each curriculum had its own unique offering, and I am grateful for the opportunity to experience them all. With every change, I made new friends, learned valuable lessons, and created countless memories.

School had it all—classes with supportive teachers, looking forward to delicious lunch boxes packed by my mom, company of amazing friends, playing sports and some inspiring mentors who saw potential in a quiet student and helped turn a spark into a flame. School became the stepping stone where I learned what it meant to be a student, a tween, and eventually a teenager.

Weekends tend to be a mix of outings, activities, and long debates about the future—what I want to do in life, where I see myself studying, and whether I should be preparing for something I haven't even thought of yet. The classic "What do you want to be when you grow up?" the question still lingers, though my answers have changed over time. Rockstar, astronaut, detective, economist—at one point, everything felt possible. The adults in my life would nod along, amused but encouraging, as if any answer could turn into reality.

Now, those questions feel more real, and so does the invisible pressure that comes with them. Maybe once in a while, the external ecosystem that we are a part of, makes me feel that who I am is being defined by our grades, achievements, and extracurriculars, many in my peer group would agree with me. Doing well is definitely very rewarding and motivating, but also overwhelming—that's why trying to balance school with everything else is the key that makes life enjoyable. Spending time with friends, diving into hobbies, going for an odd concert or two or just catching up on a show that everyone's talking about are some of the things that I enjoy. Thankfully, my mom acts as my built-in reminder to step away from the constant cycle of schoolwork, especially when exams are close—a quick outing with friends, a short snack break, a walk to clear the head, a game of tennis with my father - because sometimes, the smallest things help the most. Even some window shopping at Sephora (she knows me so well!), Dubai Mall is just next door.

At home, education isn't just important—it's at the core of everything. It fuels dinner conversations, sparks curiosity, and leads to never-ending discussions. A few winters back, the big ongoing debate in our house was which country do I want to go to for my higher studies. My parents, true to their style, are treating this decision with equal parts enthusiasm and research—comparing different colleges with similar courses, considering ratings, and discussing every possible scenario. But what makes these conversations meaningful is that they always return to the same question: Where will I feel most inspired? Which path will help me grow, not just as a student, but as a person?

Even my grandparents weigh in, reminding me through their own stories that education isn't just about academics—it's about curiosity, exploration, and finding the joy in learning itself.

For me, the process feels less like a burden and more like an adventure. It isn't about choosing the "right" or "wrong" option—it's about imagining where I can explore the subjects I love, where learning will feel exciting and meaningful. The idea that success can be defined by happiness, not just grades, makes the whole decision feel empowering. Suddenly, it isn't just about the majors and minors —it's a chance to shape the kind of journey I want, one that will challenge me in the best ways and help me truly flourish.

Amidst all this, I came across the book *I Am Malala.*

I had heard her story before—seen her name in headlines, listened to teachers describe her bravery. But reading her words, in her own voice, was something entirely different. She wrote about walking to school through the shadow of fear, knowing each step was an act of defiance. She wrote about wanting to learn, even when others wanted to take that right away.

And then, there was the line that really got me thinking: ***"If one man can destroy everything, why can't one girl change it?"***

It was a question so simple yet powerful that I had to put the book down for a moment just to let it sink in. Here I was, worrying about school systems and extracurriculars, while someone like Malala had risked everything for the chance to learn. Her story made me see the privilege in my own life in a way that felt real. It was raw, humbling, and grounding all at once.

A couple of months later, I found myself in my grandparents' home in India, a place where everything felt familiar—the warm smell of chai drifting from the kitchen, the sound of my dadi's voice as she lovingly cajoled us to eat more. As with all grandmoms, most of their love and affection is channeled through gastronomical delights - She made sure that whatever my brother and I adored eating was cooked, remembering our favorite dishes. "Have this, eat that," she'd say, ensuring our plate was never empty, her care woven into every bite.

It was the kind of place where life slowed down, where small moments stretched into quiet reflections.

That's where I first met Kajal and Priyanka.

They arrived in the afternoon, stepping into the veranda where I was curled up with Malala's book. Kajal's smile wavered for a moment before blooming brightly, while Priyanka hovered just behind her, hesitating in the shadows. Their presence was quiet yet commanding, their eyes filled with a mix of curiosity and hesitation. They had come to meet my grandparents to discuss their education—or rather, the possibility of continuing it.

As we all settled into conversation, it was Priyanka's voice that first broke the silence. She spoke about her elder sister, whose schooling had ended abruptly after the 10th grade because her family couldn't afford the fees. Her sister was married off shortly after, and Priyanka feared the same fate awaited her if help didn't come soon. She paused, glanced down, and then looked back up with quiet determination. "If I can just finish school, I know I can change my family's life," she said.

Her words really hit me. Sitting there, I couldn't help but think of Malala's story—her fight for education in the face of unimaginable odds. Yet here, right in front of me, was a girl facing her own battle, one shaped by financial constraints and societal expectations.

Kajal's story was no less moving. She had switched from a private school to a neighbourhood school after her family could no longer afford the fees. The new school was far from her home, and the long commute presented constant challenges. For girls like Kajal, long journeys to school often carry risks that go beyond physical exhaustion—they face unsafe routes, lack of proper transportation, and societal stigmas that discourage parents from sending daughters to distant schools. These concerns are compounded by the lack of basic infrastructure, such as proper security or gender-sensitive facilities, which makes the decision to continue education even harder for families. Still, her love for science kept her going. "I want to become a doctor," she said with a shy smile. "But first, I need to finish school."

The more they talked, the more I felt something change in me. It wasn't just their words—it was the way they spoke with so much strength and clarity about their dreams, even with all the challenges they were facing.

For girls like Kajal and Priyanka, just as talented and determined as me, the question "What do you want to be when you grow up?" didn't come with endless possibilities. Their answers were tied to one simple thing—whether they could even stay in school. Their education, and their future, wasn't in their hands. It all depended on circumstances they couldn't control.

For the first time, I truly understood the human side of the stories I'd only read about. These weren't distant struggles unfolding in another part of the world; they were right here, sitting across from me, their hopes and challenges laid bare in a way that was impossible to ignore.

As the conversation wound down, I looked at Priyanka and Kajal and thought about the line from Malala's book that had stayed with me: *"Why can't one girl change it?"*

In that moment, the question felt less like an abstract challenge and more like a call to action. Meeting them wasn't just a chance encounter; it was a moment that would shape the choices I made going forward.

And I knew, deep down, that doing nothing wasn't an option.

The Day It All Changed

Meal times in our family have always been more than just about food—they're a chance to share stories, make plans, and connect. It was during one such dinner, with the clinking of plates and hands reaching for food, that what began as a casual conversation took an unexpected turn. My grandparents were recounting their colony tales, and my parents were tossing around ideas for a short trip to escape the brutal North Indian summer.

But that evening, the focus shifted to something far more meaningful: Kajal and Priyanka, and whether we could support their education. My grandparents explained what sponsoring them would entail—school fees, uniforms, books, and ensuring they had the tools to keep learning. On the surface, it seemed simple enough: a financial commitment. But the more they talked, the more I began to understand that this wasn't just about money. It was about standing behind their dreams, about believing in them when so many others wouldn't. It was about responsibility.

As I listened, Malala's words from her book echoed in my mind. I'd just finished reading it a few days before, and there was a passage that had stuck with me—one where she described the sacrifices her father made to ensure she could go to school. *"My father believed in me,"* she wrote. *"He said I had a right to education, just as much as any boy."*

That belief had carried Malala through threats, violence, and unimaginable odds. And now, sitting at the dinner table, I realized we had a chance to offer that same belief to Kajal and Priyanka.

The more my grandparents spoke, the stronger the urge grew within me. I wanted to help. I hadn't said it aloud yet, but the decision was forming in my mind, solidifying with every word they spoke. How could I not? Kajal and Priyanka deserved the chance to dream as boldly as I did.

Without thinking much more, I finally spoke. "I want to help," I said, my voice quiet but certain.

My dad's voice broke through my thoughts, steady and deliberate. "Are you sure this is something you're ready for?" he asked, looking straight at me. His question caught me off guard—not because I didn't want to help, but because it made me pause. This wasn't about casually donating to a cause and moving on. It was about committing to a relationship. It was about showing up—not just once, but again and again—when things got hard, when doubts crept in, when the challenges felt bigger than the solutions.

I nodded, swallowing the lump in my throat. "Yes," I want to sponsor their education through my pocket money. I said, my voice firmer than I felt inside. It wasn't confidence— it was pure conviction. I told my dad I wanted to support

Kajal and Priyanka in every way I could. He looked at me and said, "The girls don't just need financial support; they need someone to talk to as well." Without hesitation, I replied, "Of course. I want to support them emotionally and financially." Because while I didn't have all the answers, I knew this: Kajal and Priyanka deserved the chance to dream as boldly as I did. And if the means to make that happen could be arranged, how could we not?

The next few days were a blur of activity. My grandparents, who co-founded GyaanJyoti, the trust that worked with girls in the region, began figuring out the logistics. The fees were arranged to be paid directly to the school, and my parents coordinated with the organization for the rest. But I wanted to do more than just transfer money. I wanted to be part of the details—the things that would make Kajal and Priyanka feel seen and valued.

I remembered a passage from *I Am Malala,* where she talked about her first day back at school after the attack. Her friends had decorated her desk with flowers and notes, and though her injuries made it hard for her to sit or write, she felt a deep sense of belonging. "They made me feel like I mattered," she wrote. That line stayed with me. I wanted Kajal and Priyanka to feel the same way—that their education was something we genuinely cared about.

When the new uniforms arrived, I couldn't help but run my hands over the crisp fabric. The notebooks smelled faintly of fresh paper, the way they always did at the start of a school year. For me, these things had always been normal. Expected. But for Kajal and Priyanka, they were extraordinary.

The day we delivered the supplies is one I'll always remember. Kajal and Priyanka stood there, wide-eyed, taking it all in. Priyanka reached out cautiously, her fingers brushing the edge of a textbook before hugging it tightly to her chest like it was the most precious thing in the world. Her eyes filled with tears as she looked up at me and whispered, "Avni didi, you know this is the first time I have touched fresh books. I have always used books that have been passed down by multiple people." Then she simply added, "Thank you." Those two words carried so much—gratitude, hope, and something deeper I can't quite put into words.

Kajal couldn't stop grinning as she checked out the uniform. "I'll actually look like a real student now," she said with a soft laugh. Her excitement was contagious, and for a moment, it felt like the weight of everything had lifted. It wasn't just about school anymore—it was about dignity, about giving them something to hold onto as they faced what was ahead..

I thought of Malala again and the ripple effect she often spoke about. "When you educate one girl," she wrote, "you change her family, her community, her world." Standing there with Kajal and Priyanka, I felt the truth of those words in a way I never had before. This wasn't just about their futures. It was about creating a shift—a small one, maybe, but one that mattered.

As they walked away that day, books and uniforms in hand, I realized something else. This wasn't just their journey. It was ours too. Sponsorship wasn't the end of the story—it was the beginning of a relationship, one that would teach me as much as it would support them.

And for the first time in a long time, I felt a sense of clarity. Malala's words had inspired me to ask, "Why can't one girl change it?" But now, I was beginning to understand that the question wasn't just about them. It was about all of us. Together.

Reflections on Growth and Resilience

As I spent more time with Kajal and Priyanka, I began to see the layers of their lives, their struggles, and their hopes unfold in ways I hadn't anticipated. Kajal, at just 14 years old, radiated a curiosity that was both infectious and humbling. Her love for science wasn't the kind that came from textbooks alone; it was born from a genuine desire to understand how things worked. She told me about her favorite experiments at school—mixing substances to see chemical reactions, observing insects in the garden, how our organs worked cohesively, and sketching constellations she'd read about. Her excitement was so real, it almost made you forget the challenges she dealt with every single day.

Getting to school wasn't easy for Kajal. It was far away, and just the journey could've been enough to make most people give up. She woke up before dawn each morning, squeezed into crowded rickshaws, and walked a long, unsafe road just to make it to class. Sometimes the roads were littered with garbage. Her parents were always worried, but they knew how much her education meant to her. For Kajal, it wasn't just about going to school—it was about fighting against the limits her circumstances tried to set. "One day, I'll wear a doctor's white coat." she told me with this quiet but determined smile. For her, that white lab coat wasn't just a career goal—it was a symbol of strength and fairness in a world that hadn't always been kind to her.

Priyanka, on the other hand, had a quieter presence, but her resilience spoke volumes. She often talked about her older sister, who had been forced to leave school after the 10th grade and was married soon after. "That could have been me," Priyanka said softly one afternoon. Her voice didn't waver, but her eyes betrayed the weight of what she carried. Unlike her sister, Priyanka had managed to stay in school, and she was determined to go even further. "If I can finish college, I'll prove that girls in our community can achieve more," she added. She wasn't just dreaming for herself; she was setting an example, showing others what was possible when you refused to give up.

Hearing their stories made me reflect deeply on my own life. While I spent my days debating whether to register for a MUN, preparing for the next round of the World Scholar's Cup, or planning a weekend outing to get my nails done with friends—small decisions that felt significant at the time—Kajal and Priyanka spent theirs fighting to hold on to the opportunity to learn. It was humbling to realize that the things I took for granted—access to books, safe classrooms, supportive teachers—were privileges that so many girls like them could only dream of.

It reminded me of a line from Malala's book: **"When the whole world is silent, even one voice becomes powerful."**

Kajal and Priyanka's voices weren't loud, but they carried the weight of dreams that demanded to be heard. And as our conversations continued, I began to see how their dreams weren't just theirs alone. They were intertwined with the hopes of their families and the aspirations of other girls in their community who watched them with quiet admiration.

Over time, our connection deepened. What started as a formal sponsorship transformed into something far more personal. Kajal would eagerly share updates about her Biology projects, her excitement bubbling over as she described new things she'd learned. Priyanka, in her thoughtful way, spoke about her favorite professors and the subjects that inspired her the most. These moments of sharing, of celebrating their small victories became some of the most meaningful parts of my own journey.

There was one day in particular that stands out in my memory. Priyanka had just completed an important exam, and she messaged me first to ask if she could call. Just calling whenever wasn't really possible—they only had one phone, and it belonged to her father. She had to wait until he came home from work to make the call. When she finally called, her excitement was palpable. "I was so nervous," she admitted, "but I kept thinking about how much this means—not just for me, but for my family." Her voice was steady, but there was a quiet joy in it, a pride that was impossible to miss. It wasn't just an exam for her; it was a step toward proving what she had always believed—that education could change everything.

Kajal's milestones were equally inspiring. She once showed me a sketch she'd made of a science experiment she hoped to try one day. It was simple, just pencil on paper, but it represented so much more—a glimpse into her imagination, her curiosity, her determination to keep learning no matter the obstacles.

Through them, I began to understand that education isn't just about academics. It's about unlocking potential and opening doors to possibilities that might otherwise remain closed. And in doing so, it changes everyone involved—students, families, and even those of us lucky enough to support them.

Looking back, I realized that sponsoring them wasn't an act of charity—it was an act of belief. Belief in their ability to rise above their circumstances, to create change not just for themselves but for those around them.

They weren't just pursuing their dreams—they were redefining what was possible for every girl who watched them, for every parent who wondered if it was worth the sacrifice, and for every community that doubted the power of education for the girl child. And as they moved forward, step by step,

I felt privileged to walk alongside them, learning as much from their journey as they had from mine.

Small Steps, Big Changes

As Priyanka settled into college life at SD College in Panipat, her updates became small windows into a world she was steadily carving out for herself. I remember the day she called me during my winter break. Her voice carried an excitement that made me smile before she'd even said a word. She spoke about her professors—how they challenged her thinking and inspired her to aim higher. "They make you see things differently," she said, her tone filled with admiration. She described how her days were spent soaking in lectures, preparing for exams, and dreaming of teaching one day.

It felt surreal listening to her. This was the same girl who had once been on the brink of dropping out, her future teetering on circumstances beyond her control. And now, she sounded like any other college student—filled with dreams, aspirations, and the determination to make them real.

"I'll never forget what you did for me," she said, her voice quieter now. "Without the scholarship, I'd have been married after 10th grade. But now, I can see a different future for myself." Her words stayed with me, a reminder of how impactful even small steps could be.

Kajal's love for science extended beyond herself. She would return home and share her learning with her younger siblings, simplifying complex ideas into something they could grasp. It wasn't just about her education—it was about showing her family what was possible.

"They're so proud of her," her mother once shared with my grandparents. Kajal wasn't just learning for herself—she was showing her family how education could make a difference for all of them.

Their progress wasn't without challenges. Priyanka spoke candidly about the pressures she felt—not just academically but in balancing the expectations of her community. "Sometimes, it feels like everyone's watching," she said. "But then I remember why I'm doing this." Her resilience was humbling, a testament to the strength she had carried all along.

In these moments, I realized something bigger was happening. Education wasn't just transforming their lives—it was rewriting the story for everyone around them.

Think about how powerful that is. To change an entire community's idea of what's possible. To see a little girl lead the way, fueled by belief in her dreams—and by someone else believing in her too.

That's the magic of giving. That's the kind of impact a single act of generosity can have. It's not just support—it's a spark that ignites lasting change.

Priyanka's achievements inspired other girls in her neighborhood to think beyond the traditional confines of what was expected of them. She began mentoring younger girls, sharing her journey and encouraging them to stay in school. And coming from someone who had walked the same uncertain paths they were on, her words carried weight.

For Kajal, the changes were more subtle but equally significant. She started influencing her younger siblings, showing them the importance of persistence and education. I remember her mother's pride as she shared how Kajal had become a role model within their family. Victories like helping her younger brother solve a tough math problem became moments of celebration.

I've realized that these seemingly small steps—a scholarship, a conversation, a moment of encouragement—are anything but small. They're the foundation of something much larger. Malala's words echoed in my mind once more: "When you educate a girl, you educate a generation." Through Kajal and Priyanka, I witnessed that truth unfold in real-time.

Supporting them wasn't just about helping them chase their dreams—it taught me what it really means to believe in someone. It wasn't focused on big, dramatic changes. It centered on small steps. Yet in those small steps, I saw the start of something bigger—for Kajal, for Priyanka, and for everyone they inspired along the way, including me.

(Not So) Small Transformations

In the subsequent days that followed, Kajal and Priyanka's lives were transformed from not going to school to being at the center of what they had been striving for. My conversations with Priyanka became shared stories of her campus experiences. Her words brimmed with excitement as she spoke about her professors and the subjects she loved. Political history quickly became her favorite. "I want to show the girls in my community that education can change everything," she said with a confident smile. "Not just as a way out, but as a way forward."

Of course, that's exactly what she did. One day, the shy teenage girl from next door came over after hearing the news about her college acceptance. "Didi, do you think I could go to college too?" she asked, her voice barely above a whisper. Priyanka's eyes sparkled with excitement as she replied, "Why not? If I can do it, so can you."

That moment opened up a world of possibilities that the girl had never dared to imagine before.

Kajal's perseverance had become a source of pride within her family. She told me about helping her younger siblings with their homework and teaching them math problems she had learned at school. "They're smarter than I was at their age," she'd say, laughing, but I could hear the pride in her voice.

Her parents, who once worried about whether educating their daughter was worth the sacrifices, now looked to her as proof that those sacrifices were meaningful. Her younger brother, inspired by her journey, had begun taking his studies more seriously, determined to follow her example.

Hearing these stories made me reflect deeply on the concept of change. Sometimes, it was as simple as one conversation, one act of kindness, one decision to believe in someone. And those small moments, repeated and shared, could lead to transformations that extended far beyond what any of us could predict.

Even within my own family, I began to see the influence of supporting Kajal and Priyanka. My parents, who had always valued education, became even more vocal advocates for girls' education. They'd share Kajal and Priyanka's stories with friends and relatives, encouraging them to contribute to similar causes. A few of our family friends started sponsoring girls through GyaanJyoti, inspired by what they saw in Priyanka and Kajal's progress.

It wasn't just about inspiring others. Supporting them completely changed how I saw what I could do—not just with my privilege, but with conviction. It felt like a mission in action.

As I thought about their journeys and the changes they were creating, I felt an overwhelming sense of gratitude. Gratitude for the chance to be part of their lives, for the lessons they taught me, and for the opportunity to witness the incredible power of education. And as much as I had hoped to change their lives, I realized they had changed mine too.

Looking at what they've accomplished, I'm reminded of something my grandfather once said: "Change doesn't happen all at once. It starts small, like a seed. But with time, it grows into something strong, something that lasts."

Kajal and Priyanka are those seeds, and watching them grow has been one of the greatest privileges of my life. But what I've come to understand is that their growth is part of something much bigger—a mission that keeps moving forward with every small step we take.

The influence of helping one girl can reach far and wide, shaping not just her future but the future of everyone around her. It's a reminder that change doesn't require grand gestures or perfect circumstances—it only needs a willingness to whether it's supporting education, mentoring someone, or simply encouraging a child to dream bigger, every small effort matters.

This is what "Mission in Motion" means: the belief that our actions, however small, can spark something powerful and lasting. It's about moving forward together—each step building on the last—to create a world where every child, every girl, has the chance to thrive.

So, as you finish this chapter, I hope you'll ask yourself: What's the next step I can take? Maybe it's supporting a cause close to your heart, volunteering your time, or sharing a story that inspires someone else to act. Whatever it is, know that even the smallest step can set a mission in motion.

***"Education is the greatest hope of our time. It gives hope to the hopeless and creates chances for those without."*—*Kofi Annan.*

Because when we believe in someone, when we take that first step to support them, we aren't just changing one life—we're creating possibilities for countless others. And that's the kind of change that lasts.

CHAPTER 4

Beneath the Surface

I once saw a video of a little girl trying to push open a heavy wooden door.

She couldn't have been more than five or six, standing in front of this massive door that towered over her, its worn wooden surface etched with years of use. She stared at it for a second, like she was sizing it up, and then she went for it. Pressing her tiny hands against the wood, she leaned in with all her weight, her sneakers squeaking against the floor as she pushed. Her face scrunched up, cheeks red with effort, but the door didn't even budge. Not an inch.

She stepped back, frustrated, and stared at it again like she was challenging it to a fight. Then she wiped her hands on her dress and tried again. This time, she threw everything into it—her face furrowed, her breaths short and sharp, her feet shuffling forward in an awkward dance of defiance against the immovable. Still, nothing. The door stood as solid as the walls around it. It was like watching someone try to move a mountain with their bare hands.

A few more tries. A little more desperation each time. Then, finally, her shoulders slumped. She pounded a small fist against the wood—one last attempt, one last plea. But the door didn't care.

After what felt like forever—seriously, the struggle was almost painful to watch - a shadow fell across her. A man stepped beside her, watching for a moment before reaching out, turning the handle, and pushing the door open with a quiet groan. No struggle. No effort. It had never been locked in the first place. She'd been pushing instead of pulling.

The girl froze, her eyes wide.

For a moment, she didn't move.

She had spent so much time fighting this door, convincing herself it was impossible, that now—when the path was suddenly open—she hesitated.

Did she trust him? Did she trust that stepping forward wouldn't lead to something worse?

She blinked, hesitated a second longer, then stepped inside. Slowly. Like she wasn't sure if she'd won or lost.

I don't even remember where I saw that video—probably scrolling on my phone during break, another random clip buried in an algorithm throwing everything at me, from memes to news to life hacks I'd never use. But for some reason, it stuck. Maybe because it reminded me of how life sometimes feels—like you're pushing with everything you've got against something that just won't move… only to realize you've been missing the handle all along.

I think about that a lot when it comes to these girls' education.

Sometimes, the doors holding them back aren't locked. They've just been told for so long that they can't open them that they stop trying. Or they don't even reach for the handle because they assume it won't budge. And when someone like GyaanJyoti steps in—not to force the door open, but to show them how—it changes everything.

But the truth is, even when the door opens, stepping through isn't always easy.

Because sometimes, when you've spent your whole life believing something is out of reach, being told otherwise doesn't feel like freedom—it feels like a trick. A risk.

What if it's not safe on the other side? What if it's a trap? What if you step forward and everything collapses underneath you?

I remember hearing about one girl—a bright student sponsored by GyaanJyoti, who had been excelling in school. She loved maths. She wanted to be a engineer. Everyone believed she would go far.

And then, one day, she was gone.

Her family had pulled her out of school. The same people who once supported her education had arranged her marriage instead. She never got to finish.

That story stuck with me because it wasn't a failure of effort. GyaanJyoti had done everything right. They had provided funding, guidance, and encouragement. But sometimes, the problem isn't just money—it's mindsets that have been passed down for generations, like an ancient, unmovable door.

And sometimes, even when you show a girl the way forward, the world around her makes sure she never walks through.

I once asked my grandparents about a question that comes up a lot in the communities they work with:

"If you have two children—a son and a daughter—but you can only afford to send one to school, who do you choose?"

For many families in India, this isn't just a hypothetical. It's reality. And most of the time, more often than not, the answer is the son.

When I first heard this, I wanted to argue. Why does it have to be a choice? Why can't both children go to school? But for some families, education isn't just about opportunity—it's about survival. A son is seen as an investment. A daughter is seen as an expense.

That was a hard truth to accept. But it also made me realize why trusts like GyaanJyoti exist—not just to provide financial aid but to shift the thinking behind choices like these.

Because, in the end, the door isn't locked. It's just waiting for someone to turn the handle.

And, just as importantly, for someone to trust that they can walk through.

The Complexities of Change

Getting a girl into school is never as simple as offering financial aid. It's not like handing over a check and watching everything fall into place. The real challenge—the exhausting, frustrating part—is convincing people that education is even worth it. That a girl sitting in a classroom is not a waste of time or money. That investing in her future doesn't come at the cost of losing her 'value' in society.

That's what my grandparents have spent years doing—not just funding education but undoing generations of the belief that girls belong anywhere but school.

Once, they met a father who refused to send his daughter to school, even when GyaanJyoti offered to cover every single cost. Fees, books, uniforms—everything. "She belongs at home," he said. "If she studies too much, who will marry her?"

I remember hearing that story and feeling this deep frustration settle in my chest. She was smart. She had potential.

And yet, none of that mattered because, to him, her worth was measured by marriage, not by knowledge.

The hardest part? He wasn't trying to be cruel. In his mind, he was protecting her in the only way he had been taught. He had grown up in a world steeped in tradition, where a girl's worth was often measured by her ability to fulfill the societal mold of a 'good wife.' In this world, too much education wasn't seen as empowerment but as a risk—a threat to her 'marriageability.' He had been raised to believe that a girl who questioned boundaries, who sought independence, or who prioritized personal ambition might face not just disapproval but outright alienation. It wasn't just about her; it was about the family, the community, and the weight of expectations passed down through generations. Stepping outside these rigid boundaries didn't just challenge norms—it could invite whispers, judgment, and the risk of being cast out from the very fabric of belonging.

For so many people just like him, tradition is not simply a guideline or something passed down through generations in good faith; it becomes a survival mechanism. He thought he was shielding her from the storms of a world that had little tolerance for those who strayed too far from its rules.

And it's not just fathers—it's mothers too. I've seen women, the very ones who have lived through the weight of constrained choices, become the staunchest enforcers of these rules. These are women who, in theory, should empathize most with the need for freedom and agency, yet they uphold the same structures that once limited them.

Why? Because this is what they've been taught. This is what their mothers and grandmothers before them were taught. It's a cycle deeply embedded in cultural expectations, where tradition is often mistaken for morality, and obedience is framed as virtue. To step outside these norms, to challenge them, requires more than personal courage—it demands a reckoning with generations of social conditioning. Yet these norms are so pervasive, so deeply ingrained in their communities, that breaking free can feel like turning your back on your heritage, your community, perhaps even your family.

The world around them has reinforced these roles so consistently, so convincingly, that to question them often feels like questioning your place in it.

This is one of the biggest challenges trusts like GyaanJyoti face—convincing families that education isn't just something nice for their daughters but something necessary. That it doesn't threaten their future—it secures it. It doesn't happen overnight. Change, especially when it comes to deeply rooted traditions and cultural expectations, takes time. It takes countless conversations, shared lived experiences, and moments of vulnerability. It takes trust built not through grand gestures but through consistent actions—showing up, listening, understanding. And sometimes, it takes proof— proof that education can empower, proof that stepping outside the norm can lead to something better.

My grandparents have spent years walking this delicate balance with these communities. They've sat with families, heard their fears, and respected their values while gently challenging the norms that hold their daughters back. Slowly, they've earned the trust of parents who, for generations, believed a girl's place was in the home. So when my grandparents say, "Let your daughter study," it's not just words.

It's a plea backed by years of connection and an unshakable belief in the power of education—one that makes people pause, reflect, and, more often than not, listen.

And even then, it doesn't always work. Some families still pull their daughters out of school. Others never let them start in the first place. Because change isn't just about providing something better—it's about helping people believe that better is possible. That takes time.

Like I said, beliefs rooted in generations don't shift overnight. For many families, sending their daughters to school isn't just a financial decision—it's a cultural one. There's a fear of breaking tradition, of stepping into unknown territory. What will the neighbors say? What will the relatives think? For many, the idea of educating girls isn't just seen as unnecessary—it's seen as risky.

Then there's the issue of money. Education isn't free, and even with financial aid, the costs can feel impossible for families already stretched thin. In rural communities, a family may have to choose between sending a child to school or paying for basics like food and clothing. And most of the time, when that choice has to be made, it's the daughters who lose out. Boys are seen as the priority, the future breadwinners, while girls are expected to stay home, help with chores, and prepare for marriage.

When GyaanJyoti was first launched, my grandparents tried to address part of the problem by offering financial support. They started small, giving 500 rupees a month to help underprivileged girls attend school. It wasn't much, but it was something. For many parents, it was just enough to tip the balance, just enough to make them say yes. That 500 rupees became more than money—it became a vote of confidence in their daughters' futures. It said to those families, "Your daughters are worth it."

But then came the real challenge of scaling it. How do you take small, meaningful gestures like that and turn them into something bigger? Something sustainable? Because for every family that says yes, there are still so many more who hesitate, caught in the web of financial limitations, cultural expectations, and the simple fear of change.

And that's the hardest part—convincing them that breaking free is worth it.

Every conversation at home seemed to circle back to the same pressing questions: "How do we help more girls? How do we secure more funding?" It was an endless cycle of hope and frustration. My grandparents had big dreams—they believed in empowering young girls through education—but without a steady stream of donations, they were constantly hitting a wall. And the toughest challenge wasn't convincing people to care; it was proving that their money would actually make it to the girls who needed it most.

When Progress Stalls

In India, there's a deep-rooted skepticism around NGOs. People want to help, but they're wary. Too many stories of funds vanishing into a maze of 'administration fees' have made donors cautious. So trust became everything. Most of GyaanJyoti's sponsors weren't random strangers—they were family friends, old colleagues, and neighbors from the same community. These were people who had seen my grandparents' commitment up close, who trusted their intentions and knew that every rupee would go exactly where it was needed. Without that trust, none of this would have been possible.

Even with donations trickling in, the journey was far from smooth. Cultural and systemic barriers cropped up at every turn. One of the biggest hurdles was something we hadn't anticipated: banks. They didn't want to open accounts for the girls. In their eyes, these girls were not 'profitable'—they came from rural, economically disadvantaged backgrounds, and to the banks, they didn't represent a viable customer base. It didn't matter that the accounts were for scholarships or financial aid; we had to fight tooth and nail for every single one.

My grandparents would travel to bank branches in remote areas, armed with paperwork, determination, and a strong argument for why these girls deserve access to financial independence. They spoke to bank managers, wrote letters, and leaned on their community networks for support. It wasn't about just opening an account; it was about proving that these girls mattered, that their future was worth investing in. After years of persistence, a breakthrough finally came. A government policy allowing zero-balance accounts gave us the leverage we needed to cut through the red tape. Suddenly, the banks had no excuse to deny these girls what they rightfully deserved.

But even then, the work didn't stop. For my grandparents, this wasn't just about logistics; it was about shifting mindsets. In many parts of India, the idea of giving girls financial control is still seen as radical. Girls are often expected to contribute to household chores, marry early, and prioritize their families over their own dreams. Education—and the financial independence that comes with it—is a lifeline, but it's also a statement of defiance against generations of inequality.

What my grandparents understood so deeply was that change doesn't happen in isolation. It's not just about scholarships or donations; it's about creating an ecosystem of belief, trust and opportunity. They didn't just want to fund education—they wanted to rewrite what was possible for these young girls. It was never easy, but every account opened, every girl who stayed in school, and every donor who placed their trust in this mission felt like a small victory in a much larger fight. And in those moments, the questions at the dinner table shifted slightly—from "How do we help more girls?" to "What's next?" And then, there's the question of what happens after school. For many families, the real struggle isn't allowing their daughters to study—it's what comes next. Higher education? A career? For countless girls, that's where the door quietly but firmly closes.

Many of the families that GyaanJyoti works with value schooling, but only to a certain extent. They're proud to see their daughters learn to read and write, even reach grade 10 or 12. But beyond that? Conversations quickly turn to questions of tradition and reputation. "Who will marry her if she studies too much?" It's not just a rhetorical question—it's a deeply entrenched fear, a reflection of cultural expectations where a girl's worth is often tied to her marriageability.

Families often prioritize income over education—girls are expected to work, cook, and prepare for marriage rather than attend school. Another barrier is the financial burden of dowry. Many parents believe a girl should start working early to save for marriage instead of "wasting time" in school. I once spoke to a mother who hesitated to send her daughter to university. "If we spend too much on her education, we won't have enough for her dowry," she explained.

I remember sitting in on a conversation between my grandparents and a father whose daughter had been supported by GyaanJyoti's financial aid program. She had excelled in school, her teachers believed she could thrive in college, and my grandparents gently encouraged him to consider letting her take that next step. But he shook his head, unyielding. "That's enough education for a girl," he said firmly. "She has learned to read, to write, to understand the world around her. That's good. But now it's time to think about her future— about marriage, about settling down."

Counselling workshop organised by GyaanJyoti to encourage parents to enroll meritorious girls to continue studying

Funding and donations are vital first steps, yes, but the journey toward change is far more complicated. There are fears rooted in decades, even centuries, of societal norms. There are whispered concerns about daughters becoming "too independent" about families losing control or respect in the community. It's a tangled web of tradition, gender roles, and expectations, and pulling at one thread often feels like pulling against the weight of history itself.

But then, there are moments of hope—small but powerful glimmers that make the struggle worthwhile. Like the girl who once thought her life would never extend beyond her tiny village and now dreams of becoming a doctor. Or the young woman whose parents had dismissed school as unnecessary but who now tutors her younger siblings, telling them, with quiet conviction, that education will change their lives.

These moments are rare and fragile, but they're proof that progress is possible.

For my grandparents and for so many others working to champion girls' education, these victories are what keep them going. Because for every girl who sits in a classroom, and learns to imagine a life bigger than the one defined for her, the world shifts just a little. It's a reminder that even when change feels impossibly slow—even when it feels like a single drop in an ocean—it still matters.

Every girl who gets an education is living, breathing proof that the world doesn't have to stay the same. It can be different. It can be better.

And step by step, bit by bit, it will be.

"I alone cannot change the world,

but I can cast a stone across

the waters to create many ripples"

—Mother Teresa

Setbacks

Change isn't linear. It doesn't follow a neat, straight path from problem to solution. It surges forward, pauses, hesitates—and sometimes, it unravels entirely. Progress often feels like a delicate thread, easily pulled apart by forces beyond control.

I used to believe that getting a girl into school was the hardest part. That once she had books in her hands, a desk to sit at, and the glimmer of a future in her mind, she was safe. That as long as the funding was there, as long as the school doors were open, she would stay. That she would succeed. But change doesn't work that way. It's far more complex, and far more fragile, especially when it comes to generational cycles and deeply ingrained norms.

There was a girl—I still remember her name, though I would not like to mention it here. Her laugh carried through the classroom, and her eyes lit up when she spoke about her dreams. She wasn't just smart; she was brilliant. One of the brightest in her class, always scoring at the top. She wanted to be a doctor—not just because she loved science, but because she wanted to help people in her village, where doctors were few and far between. For a while, it seemed possible. She studied harder than anyone, and stayed late after school, and her teachers believed in her. We all did.

But then, one day, she wasn't in class. At first, her absence seemed temporary—maybe she was unwell, maybe there was a family emergency. Days passed. Then weeks. Eventually, the reality surfaced: her family had decided it was time for her to marry. She was barely sixteen.

I still remember the moment I heard the news. It felt like a punch to the stomach.

We had done everything right. How could this still happen?

The school was there. The support was there. The funding, the encouragement, the opportunities—it was all there. And yet, none of it had been enough to outweigh the immovable force of expectation. The invisible current of tradition pulling her away from everything she had worked for.

She had seen it coming. That's what hit me the hardest. She knew. She must have. Looking back, I realized how she carried herself in the months prior. She worked tirelessly, but there was a quiet restraint in her joy and a distance in her determination. It was as if she never let herself fully believe her success was hers to hold on to. She climbed higher and higher, but all the while, she must have known the ladder beneath her could be pulled away at any moment.

And she wasn't wrong. For generations, girls like her have watched the same story unfold. They've watched older sisters, cousins, and neighbors excel, only to have their futures cut short. They've seen education treated as a temporary indulgence, a privilege that could vanish the moment tradition or necessity demanded it.

In some communities, a girl's success isn't just her own; it belongs to her family. And that success can feel like a threat—challenging norms, defying roles, and raising questions that many aren't ready to answer. For her parents, marrying her off wasn't an act of cruelty; it was an act of survival, a way to ensure her security in a world where a single misstep, a single deviation from the expected path, could bring shame or hardship.

And yet, the cost of that survival is devastating. It robs her of her agency, her dreams, and her future. It reinforces the quiet understanding among so many girls that no matter how hard they try, no matter how much they achieve, their futures aren't entirely their own.

For some families, education is not dismissed—it's simply out of reach. In homes where every meal is uncertain, where financial strain is a daily reality, school is often viewed as a luxury rather than a necessity. When faced with the choice between sending a daughter to school or ensuring the family's immediate survival, education becomes an afterthought.

And the heartbreaking truth? These girls understand this.

They don't beg to stay in school. They don't fight back. Not because they don't care but because they know what their families are up against. They've seen their mothers make impossible sacrifices and watched older sisters leave behind their dreams without protest. They have learned, too early, that survival means compromise. So when their time comes, they do what they've been conditioned to do: they step aside quietly, without complaint.

This is why the battle for education isn't just about access—it's about permanence. It's about ensuring that no one can take that education away from them once it's given.

It's about redefining it not as a borrowed privilege but as an untouchable right.

I used to think progress was about fighting against entrenched beliefs, a head-on clash with tradition. But over time, I've realized that sometimes progress isn't about fighting at all. It's about enduring. It's about creating systems and opportunities that outlast the barriers standing in their way.

Because traditions don't disappear overnight. Cultural norms and generational poverty don't simply fade because an NGO secures funding or starts a campaign. These forces are deeply ingrained in daily life.

Change, real change, is slow and challenging. But it's also unstoppable.

Every girl who stays in school—who refuses to let her education slip through her fingers—becomes part of something far larger than herself. She becomes a living challenge to the status quo, a seed of possibility planted where hope is scarce. Each one of these girls represents a quiet, profound victory in a landscape where losses are all too common.

This is why NGOs and trusts like GyaanJyoti don't focus solely on getting girls into classrooms. That's just the first step. The real work, the harder work, lies in keeping them there. Creating conditions where education isn't so easily taken from them. Addressing the subtle, systemic forces that pull them away—whether it's the expectation to look after younger siblings, the pressure to marry young, or the sheer weight of economic necessity. GyaanJyoti works to make education sustainable for these girls, something they can hold onto even when the world around them is telling them to let it go.

There are days when this mission feels impossible. When it feels like no matter how much we push forward, the cycles of poverty and tradition drag us one step back. Each girl lost to these forces is a pain that lingers. It's a reminder of how deeply ingrained these challenges are.

But then there are the victories. The girls who stay. The ones who hold onto their education with quiet determination, even when everything conspires against them. These are the girls who remind us why we fight, why we endure. Their resolve inspires us to keep going, to believe in a future where they are not exceptions but the norm.

One day, there will be more girls in that category than not. One day, these cycles will break under the weight of their persistence and courage. One day, education will no longer feel like a fragile hope but a sturdy foundation for every girl, no matter her circumstances.

And that's the day the world changes.

Fighting back & Building Trust

For every girl who stays in school, there are ten more standing on the edge, waiting for a reason to leave. Some are pulled away before they even start. Some get years into their education before something—marriage, money, fear—drags them back. It's not always loud. Sometimes, it happens in silence.

One day, she's in class. The next, she's not. No announcements. No dramatic goodbyes. Just an empty desk that stays empty.

That's why the fight isn't about just getting them into school. It's about making sure they stay. And that takes more than money. It takes trust. It takes convincing. It takes something stronger than fear.

The first fight is always against doubt. Not the loud, aggressive kind, but the quiet, insidious kind—the kind that has taken root over generations. It's the doubt that makes a father hesitate before signing a school form. The kind that makes a mother, standing in her kitchen, glance at her daughter and wonder, Will this really help her? Or will it only bring her more trouble?

It's not always about resistance or rejection. People assume families don't want their daughters to study, but the truth is often far more layered. Sometimes, they do want it for her, but they've been failed by the system so many times that they no longer believe in it. They don't trust that education will protect her. They don't trust that it will secure her future or lead her to a better life. And, honestly? I can't blame them.

I've sat in rooms where mothers, speaking quietly but with conviction, recount stories of daughters who worked hard, studied diligently, and earned degrees—only to find themselves back in the same place they would have been without it. Married off. Dependent. Reduced to the same roles as those who never went to school. These are not hypothetical fears; they are lived realities. When you've seen this happen again and again, the question "What's the point?" doesn't come from ignorance—it comes from experience.

And that's where the real work begins. Not with forcing them to see things differently, but with meeting them where they are. With understanding that their fear, their hesitation, is not misplaced—it's deeply rooted in a society that has let them down time and again.

GyaanJyoti understands this. They know you can't walk into a village and demand change. You can't talk about empowerment or opportunity if those words feel like hollow promises to people who have heard them before but seen little to back them up. You have to build trust. You have to speak their language—not just in words, but in values, in stories, in shared fears and hopes.

So they start with listening. Sitting in courtyards, over cups of tea, hearing the unspoken doubts and the spoken ones. They don't dismiss the questions about marriage prospects or the concerns about whether education might make a girl too ambitious—too "difficult" to marry off. They address them head-on. Not with lectures but with practical, relatable truths. How an educated daughter can contribute financially to her family. How she can navigate a world that is changing, whether her parents want it to or not. How, in many ways, her education is not just for her—it's for them.

But trust isn't built on words alone. It needs proof, and that's where GyaanJyoti's approach stands out. They started holding seminars—but not the kind where NGO representatives stand at the front of a room with slides and statistics. Instead, they invited people from the community itself to speak. Elders, respected figures, people whose voices carried weight. A grandfather who once opposed his granddaughter's education now telling others how proud he is of her achievements. A mother who once kept her daughter at home sharing how her daughter's degree helped secure the family's finances when her husband fell ill. People didn't hear this from outsiders—they heard it from neighbors, from faces they knew and trusted.

And slowly, the questions began to change. Conversations shifted from "Who will marry her if she studies too much?" to "What colleges can she apply to?" From "What's the point?" to "What are her options?" Families began asking about scholarships, applications, about how they could support their daughters in taking the next step.

It wasn't an overnight transformation. It never is. It took time. It took patience. It took countless cups of tea and endless conversations. But most of all, it took proof—proof that education isn't just a lofty ideal but something tangible, something that could make a real, measurable difference in their lives.

The second fight is always against money.

Funding is unpredictable. Some years, donations pour in like a monsoon. Other years, it's a drought. For an NGO, waiting for perfect conditions is like waiting for rain in the desert—it may never come. If you only act when everything is in place, you never act at all.

So, you adapt.

When GyaanJyoti dreamed of starting digital literacy classes for young girls, they didn't sit around hoping a donor would swoop in with a check for new computers. Hope doesn't teach someone how to type. Instead, they got creative. They reached out to communities, asking for second-hand computers. What came back were old, dusty machines, some with missing keys, others in desperate need of repair. But they made it work.

They turned a shared room into a classroom and started with just three working computers. Three isn't much, but it was enough to begin. Soon, three computers turned into six as more donations trickled in. Then six became twelve. Now, that small room hums with life—dozens of girls, who once had never even seen a keyboard, are now confidently navigating the digital world. These aren't just skills; they're lifelines to opportunities their families never imagined.

When transportation became an issue—when parents hesitated to send daughters to school because the journey was too far or too unsafe—GyaanJyoti didn't stop. In rural areas, safety is not just a concern; it's a barrier. For many parents, the risk of harassment or harm on the way to school was enough to keep their daughters at home. But instead of shrugging and saying, Well, that's the problem, GyaanJyoti got to work.

Volunteers organized safe carpools, pooling resources to arrange for group transportation. In some areas, they flipped the model entirely—local teachers traveled to the students instead of the other way around. A small but profound change that turned the impossible into the possible.

The point wasn't perfection. It never was. It was progress.

Because if you wait for conditions to be ideal, you lose the chance to change anything at all.

But I've come to realize that the hardest thing to change isn't money or logistics—it's belief.

Belief is a mountain deeply rooted in culture, tradition, and years of lived experience. And belief doesn't shift because of arguments or statistics—it shifts because of proof.

I was reminded of this when I met a mother in a remote village who refused to send her daughter to school. She wasn't angry or defiant, just resigned. Her words echoed the same sentiment I'd heard before: "Nothing changes," she said, her voice tired rather than bitter. "We send them, and still, nothing changes. They study, and then they get married. What was the point?" This wasn't a question born of cynicism, but of a reality she had seen play out too many times.

She had seen it happen before with her neighbors, her relatives, and possibly even her older daughters. Education, in her eyes, was a mirage—a promise of a better life that never actually arrived.

But then, something shifted in her village.

Another girl, just a few years older, from the same background, had finished her education. But she didn't stop there. She found a job. A real job. Not as a maid or farmhand, but in an office—earning money, enough to support her family. That girl became a living, breathing argument against the belief that nothing changes.

For the first time, this mother saw education not as a gamble but as a gift. And just like that, she went from skeptic to advocate. Suddenly, she wasn't just sending her daughter to school; she was convincing other parents to do the same.

Nothing breaks barriers like proof.

In rural communities, where traditions are deeply entrenched, the success of one girl isn't just her victory. It's a story that ripples outward, reaching every other girl who's watching, every parent who's doubting, and every family who's waiting for proof that change is possible.

Stories change people more than speeches ever could.

Small Wins, Big Visions

Some days, it feels like the world is standing still.

For every girl who's allowed to stay in school, there's another who's pulled out to care for siblings, work in the fields, or be married off too early. For every mother who begins to question the traditions that hold her daughters back, there's another who clings to the comfort of familiar ways, fearful of what change might bring. Progress can feel like it's barely inching forward, constantly met with resistance.

But then, something shifts—quietly, subtly, yet powerfully.

A girl who once believed education wasn't for her tops her class, her confidence growing with every test she aces. A father, who once scoffed at the idea of sending his daughter to school, now boasts to neighbors about her achievements, pride glimmering in his voice. A mother, who once kept her daughters home out of fear of societal judgment, now stands her ground, passionately defending her decision to educate them—even against the backlash of relatives steeped in tradition.

It is in these small, personal victories that the seeds of transformation are planted. Suddenly, change doesn't feel so impossible anymore.

Every girl who stays in school isn't just altering the course of her own life; she's reshaping the future of her family, her community, and, ultimately, society at large. When enough girls push back against the barriers that restrict them, the balance of power shifts. Norms begin to wobble. Tradition starts to bend. And when it bends far enough, the world itself begins to pivot toward justice.

This is the vision trusts like GyaanJyoti are working toward—not just providing scholarships but dismantling a system that has existed for centuries. They're proving that education isn't charity; it's justice. It's a call to equity, a demand for fairness. It's a defiant statement that every girl, regardless of where she's born, deserves the chance to learn and thrive.

But this fight isn't GyaanJyoti's alone. Change is hard because change is unsettling. People fear what they don't know, and entrenched systems cling tightly to their hold. Yet, history shows us that when enough people stand up and demand better, change becomes inevitable.

So, how can you be part of this movement? It begins with action.

Support NGOs and trusts like GyaanJyoti in meaningful ways—not just with words of encouragement but with tangible contributions. Donations, volunteering, sharing their work—these small acts create the fuel that sustains their vital efforts.

Challenge the mindsets around you. Listen for the quiet remarks: the offhand comments that dismiss girls' ambitions as frivolous, the collective sigh of "that's just how things are." These small, seemingly harmless attitudes are part of the problem. Push back. Engage in conversations, no matter how uncomfortable they may feel. Every time you challenge these norms, you create a ripple—a ripple that might reach someone who rethinks their own perspective.

Finally, wield your voice as a tool for change whether it's within your local community, on social media, or in conversations with friends and family, every word counts. Change doesn't always start with protests or policies. Often, it starts in these everyday moments when someone chooses to speak up instead of staying silent.

The fight for girls' education is about more than textbooks and classrooms. It's about shifting generations of entrenched inequality and reimagining what's possible. Because when one girl learns, she carries her family, her community, and her future along with her. And when enough girls learn? The world changes.

Like I said, change isn't about grand gestures, and it's not always linear. But it's far from impossible. It requires more than access to schools and books—it demands confronting the cultural narratives that hold girls back. It means challenging expectations that tie their worth to roles they didn't choose. Real change takes patience, understanding, and an unrelenting belief that their futures are worth fighting for.

Because they are.

Every single time.

CHAPTER 5

Where Change Takes Root

What do you imagine change to be?

When I was younger, I thought of change as something bold and impossible to miss. I imagined fiery speeches broadcast to the world, protests surging through streets, fists raised in defiance. I pictured laws rewritten overnight, justice delivered in sweeping, dramatic strokes. Change, I thought, would always roar—a chorus of voices demanding to be heard, a force that would shake the earth beneath us.

But as I've grown, I've come to see a quieter reality. Change doesn't always arrive with the crash of cymbals or the glare of a spotlight. More often, it begins in whispers, in the smallest of moments that don't make headlines but alter lives in profound ways. It's in the spaces between words, in what is left unsaid, and in the gentle dismantling of long-held beliefs. It's not just in the marches or the speeches but in the subtle, almost invisible shifts—a prejudice that's quietly abandoned, a choice to forgive, an act of kindness that reframes someone's world.

Change resides in the mundane, in the everyday gestures we might overlook. It's about a father who once dismissed his daughter's dreams but now lingers at the back of a school meeting, arms crossed, silently listening. It's in a mother who never held a pencil herself, watching her daughter complete homework, tracing the letters with her finger, as if trying to bridge the gap between what was denied to her and what is now possible. It's about a young girl hesitating to raise her hand in class, unsure if her voice belongs there, and then deciding—yes, it does.

These moments may seem small, but in their quiet persistence, they carry the weight of generations. A father's listening is not just listening; it's a crack in the wall that once confined his daughter's world. A mother's touch on a piece of homework is not just touch; it's a bridge to a future she never imagined for herself. A girl's hand in the air is not just a hand; it's a declaration that her voice matters in a space where it was once absent.

Silence, too, tells stories. Some silences weigh heavy. The silence of a girl stitching clothes by the fire instead of reading books, her dreams of becoming a doctor folded away like unused fabric. The silence of a mother watching her daughter's path narrow into the same mold she once inhabited, a future bound by the same unyielding traditions. The silence of a classroom where an empty desk marks the absence of a girl married off before she even understood what choice could mean.

But then, there are silences that signal something else entirely. The silence before a father leans forward, intrigued by the story of a girl from a nearby village who got an education and transformed her family's fortunes. The silence before a mother sees her daughter's first paycheck and suddenly realizes that her daughter's life will not repeat her own. The silence before a girl, surrounded by women who've lived through sacrifice and struggle, dares to imagine a future larger than the one laid out for her.

These silences, these moments of hesitation and realization, are where true change begins. They ripple outward—across families, communities, and cultures—slowly, steadily, carving new paths where none existed before. They work like the patient drip of water against stone, unnoticed at first but gradually reshaping everything in their path.

In many cultures, change doesn't always arrive with confrontation. It often comes in subtle defiance, in traditions quietly bent rather than broken. A grandmother who tells stories of resilience instead of resignation. A father who begins to question the weight of dowries. A mother who teaches her daughter to read in secret, knowing fully well the risks but daring to believe that knowledge can never truly be taken away. These acts of quiet rebellion aren't less powerful just because they're less visible. They are, in their own way, revolutions.

To truly understand change, we must look beyond the grand gestures and into the quiet rhythms of daily life. It's in conversations over tea that plant the seeds of a new perspective. It's in the act of one person daring to hope differently, even when that hope feels fragile. It's in communities that find ways to heal old wounds, not through spectacle but through patience and persistence.

Change that lasts isn't always loud. It doesn't always come with applause. It grows in these small, unnoticed shifts—the hesitant gesture, the unspoken acknowledgment, the first step toward something uncharted. Over time, these moments accumulate, ripple outward, and reach places they were never meant to go. And when they do, they transform not just one life but the fabric of entire communities.

It's the way a father, once rigid in his beliefs, now listens, even if he doesn't yet agree. It's the way a mother, who never dared to dream for herself, dares to dream for her daughter. It's the way a girl, in the silence before she raises her hand, claims a space that the world told her wasn't hers—and in doing so, begins to rewrite the story for everyone who comes after her.

Change, I've learned, doesn't always roar. Often, it whispers. But if you listen closely to those whispers, you'll hear the beginning of something extraordinary.

And once it begins, nothing stays the same.

How One Girl's Education Becomes Everyone's Opportunity

The shift doesn't happen overnight. But when it does, it goes far beyond just one girl—it ripples outward. It changes how families perceive possibilities, reshapes how communities value potential, and shifts how future generations begin to see their place in the world.

When I think about this, I think of Kalpana. I met her in 2022 while volunteering through GyaanJyoti. She was 13 then, just like me, but the worlds we lived in couldn't have been more different. While I worried about school assignment deadlines and which school club to join, Kalpana was navigating a life that had already decided her path. Her days were spent at home, helping her mother with endless chores and watching over her younger siblings. She was learning how to sew intricate patterns, as her mother had, preparing for the life everyone around her assumed she would have—a life devoted to maintaining a household. In her world, childhood didn't extend into teenage years; it blurred into responsibility.

At GyaanJyoti, Kalpana had the chance to learn a few skills—a basic introduction to computers, the ability to stitch clothing for extra income, and even how to piece together sentences in English. The English lessons were a particular source of pride for her, even though she was shy about speaking up in front of others. Yet, despite these new abilities, I noticed something unsettling. No one spoke to her about what came next. There were no conversations about dreams or aspirations, no encouragement to imagine a future beyond the boundaries of her current existence. It was as if she had been conditioned to believe that dreaming too big wasn't for her—that looking beyond the immediate necessities of survival was a privilege meant for others, not girls like her.

What struck me most was how deeply ingrained these expectations were in the culture. Kalpana wasn't alone in this; she was one of countless girls growing up in a system where traditional gender roles dictated every step of their lives.

Education often took a backseat to prepare for marriage. Ambition was seen as a luxury, and independence was rarely a concept young girls were allowed to entertain.

Even when opportunities presented themselves, the weight of cultural norms often held them back, like an invisible tether tying them to the familiar, the expected.

But what I saw in Kalpana's quiet resilience gave me hope. She didn't openly defy the system—how could she when it had defined every parameter of her life? Yet, there was a flicker in her, an ember of curiosity that refused to be extinguished. It showed in the way she listened intently during group lessons, even when the heat of the room made others drowsy. It was there in the way her hands gently traced the lines of a worn-out textbook as if absorbing every word. She didn't know how to rebel, but she knew how to dream in small, quiet ways. And I couldn't help but wonder: What could Kalpana achieve if she were given more than the tools to survive? What if she were given permission to dream beyond the four walls of her home, beyond the weight of expectations her community had placed on her? What might happen if someone told her, perhaps for the first time, that her world could stretch far beyond the horizon she'd been shown?

Then, one day, everything shifted.

A career session had been organized at the trust, the kind of event that promised to plant seeds of possibility in the girls lives. It was a blazing hot afternoon, the kind where the air clung like an invisible weight, and the fans in the room barely stirred the stifling heat. The girls sat cross-legged on faded torn mats, their dupattas fanned out like bright patches of color against the dull floor. Some were visibly excited, their faces aglow with chatter and anticipation. Others seemed distracted, casting furtive glances at the door or whispering amongst themselves. Kalpana, as always, sat quietly in the back. Her posture was stiff, her fingers folded tightly in her lap. She stared down at her hands, avoiding the eyes of the speakers, as if uncertain whether she even belonged in this room of possibilities.

The session began, and the speakers—teachers, social workers, and even a former student who had gone on to become a nurse—took turns sharing their stories. Their voices floated through the room, mingling with the rustle of saris and the faint smell of vegetable curry that lingered from lunch. Samosas and laddoos were passed around, a rare treat that added to the sense of occasion. For many of the girls, the session was just another event—an escape from the monotony of their day. But Kalpana sat still, her gaze fixed somewhere between her hands and the space just in front of her as if she were listening with her entire being.

At first, she barely reacted. She had heard people talk about education and opportunity before, but those words had always felt like they were meant for someone else. Girls like her— the ones who quietly worked the grindstone of their families needs—weren't the kind of girls who broke free. Education had always been a luxury, an abstract concept that hovered just out of reach. But as the session continued, something subtle began to change. The speakers didn't just talk about opportunities; they shared stories. Stories of girls who had once sat in this very room, on these very mats, feeling the same sense of impossibility that Kalpana felt. Girls who had been told their futures were already written but who had found the courage to rewrite their destinies.

And then, for the first time, Kalpana saw proof that life could be different. It wasn't a grand revelation—it was a slow, dawning realization like sunlight breaking through clouds. After the session, she hesitated for a moment and then slowly approached me. Her voice was soft, but her words carried a weight I hadn't heard from her before. "I want to be a teacher," she said, her eyes meeting mine with a determination that startled me. "I want to do what these teachers do and improve people's lives."

It was the first time she had spoken about her future with certainty. It wasn't just an idle thought or a fleeting wish—it was something she wanted, something she believed could be real. The shift wasn't loud or dramatic. It didn't come with fanfare or applause. It was quiet, like a door unlocking in the stillness of night. But in that moment, everything changed.

Stories like Kalpana's aren't rare, but they never fail to move me. I've seen this transformation happen again and again, each time as remarkable as the first. It starts with the smallest of wins—like a girl scoring well on a test she once thought was beyond her. Or a father, for the first time, stepping into a school meeting to ask about his daughter's progress, his questions tentative but important. Or a mother, who has never held a pencil, watching her daughter read a letter aloud and realizing, in that moment, the immense power of education.

In a society where tradition often dictates the limits of a girl's life, these victories aren't just personal—they are revolutionary.

They ripple outward, challenging norms and expanding the boundaries of what's possible, not just for one girl but for her entire community. Kalpana's story is one of many, but it reminds me why we do this work. It reminds me how much can change when a girl is given not just the tools but the permission to dream. And in every quiet shift, every small step forward, there is the spark of something extraordinary.

But there are also moments when the shift happens suddenly, like a light turning on. I've seen parents who were once adamant about keeping their daughters at home suddenly reconsider after meeting someone whose daughter's education changed their family's future. I've heard stories of girls who thought school was pointless until they saw an older girl from their village graduate, get a job, and send money back home. These moments matter because they show that education isn't just personal—it's something that can be passed on.

At GyaanJyoti, I've witnessed firsthand the profound, long-term ripple effects of empowering girls through education. There was one young girl who, after completing her studies, took the bold step of starting her own small business. It wasn't just a personal success—she used the money she earned to ensure her younger siblings stayed in school, breaking the cycle of limited opportunities for her entire family. Then there was another girl who returned to her village to teach. She became not just an educator but a mentor, a role model for younger students who had never before seen a teacher who looked like them—someone who shared their struggles and dreams. These stories are more than anecdotes; they're living proof of a universal truth: when you educate one girl, you don't just change her life—you transform the lives of everyone around her. Her success becomes her family's her village's and ultimately, her community's.

I often find myself reflecting on how starkly different this is from my own life in Dubai. Here, education isn't just accessible—it's a certainty, an expectation embedded into the fabric of our daily lives. It's never a question of whether we'll study—it's simply a given. We're surrounded by some of the best resources in the world: state-of-the-art facilities, rich extracurricular programs, textbooks, libraries, and mentors at every turn. Our biggest challenges? Choosing the right major, acing exams or deciding on a career path. But for the girls I've met through GyaanJyoti, education is a privilege, not a right. It's something they have to fight for, often against forces far beyond their control—poverty, rigid social norms, gender bias, and even physical danger. Something as seemingly small as the cost of a school uniform, the absence of proper sanitary products, or a lack of bus fare can mean the difference between staying in school or dropping out entirely.

These barriers are not just logistical—they are deeply cultural. In many rural areas, a girl's education is still seen as secondary to household responsibilities or marriage prospects. Her dreams are often silenced before they can even take root. Despite this, what amazes me most is their resilience. For so many of these girls, the stakes are infinitely higher, yet they continue to chase the chance to learn with an almost unshakable determination. Their hope, their refusal to give up, is humbling. It forces me to confront my own privilege and asks a simple but profound question: if they refuse to back down in the face of so much adversity, how can I not do everything in my power to support them?

The contrast doesn't frustrate me—it fuels me. It gives me purpose. Because I know that for every girl who is forced to leave school, dozens more are still holding onto hope, clinging to the belief that education can deliver them from the cycle of hardship they've known all their lives.

Change is slow, often agonizingly so. It requires patience, persistence, and an unwavering belief in the process. But when change does come, it's transformative. It doesn't just lift up one girl—it shifts the trajectory of entire families, villages, and communities. A single educated girl becomes a beacon, a force capable of rewriting the narrative for those around her. And that's why this work, this fight for education, will always be worth it. Because every small victory is a step toward something bigger—a future where education is not a privilege, but a right for every girl, no matter where she's born or the obstacles she faces.

The Power of Role Models

But for change to truly take root, it takes more than just education. It takes inspiration. It takes role models. In a country like India, where traditions run deep and societal structures can be rigid, role models have the power to crack open possibilities for those who dare to dream.

I used to think role models were the big names in history books—activists, CEOs, world leaders, Olympic athletes. People who had "made it," whose stories proved what was possible.

But working with GyaanJyoti shifted my perspective. In the fields, towns, and cities, role models are everywhere— older sisters fighting for their education, mothers encouraging their daughters to dream bigger, and teachers going the extra mile. These everyday heroes quietly plant the seeds for change, proving that greatness isn't always loud or headline-worthy.

True role models don't always stand in the spotlight. Often, they don't even realize they're inspiring anyone at all. But they are. Change doesn't just come from the celebrated; it comes from the determined actions of those who believe something different is possible.

Many times, I think of Sakshi and Varsha's mom, Sunita. She never went to school, never learned to read or write, and never had the opportunities she's now ensuring her daughters have. But that hasn't stopped her from becoming a leader in her own way. She teaches women in her village how to sew so they can earn their own money. She volunteers with Chetna Parivaar, Panipat chapter (another NGO), working with young children and making sure they have the foundation she never had. She's not famous. There won't be articles written about her or awards in her name. But she's changing lives.

She is proving, every single day, that knowledge—whether it's reading a book or learning a skill—has the power to shift entire communities. And the children she teaches? They'll go on to teach others. That's how change grows.

Then there's Aarti at GyaanJyoti who never got to attend university, but she made sure her younger siblings did. She taught them how to read, helped them with their schoolwork, and pushed them to dream beyond what they had been told was possible. She didn't let her own missed opportunity define what was possible for the people around her because role models don't always look like the ones we expect. Not your sparkly awards or glamorous - or rather, glamourised activists. Sometimes, they're simply people who refuse to let circumstances decide the course of their lives—and, in doing so, they inspire others to do the same.

When I first read *I Am Malala*, what stood out to me most wasn't just Malala's courage—it was the unwavering support of her father. He believed in her, fought for her, and gave her the confidence to use her voice in a world that tried to silence her. That kind of support is rare. Most girls at GyaanJyoti don't have parents who encourage their education. Many have to fight for their right to learn, sometimes completely on their own.

But I've seen that strength come from unexpected places. Like the girl whose parents wanted her to drop out, but a teacher convinced them otherwise. He didn't argue or demand. He simply showed them her grade 10 report card—over 80% in her exams. He told them, "She has a gift. If you let her continue, she could go far." That was enough to make them hesitate. Enough to make them reconsider. And sometimes, that's all it takes.

Or the younger girls who see an older student from their village get into college, and suddenly, they start asking different questions. They start wondering if maybe they could do the same. They start refusing to settle.

Resilience doesn't always come from support. Sometimes, it comes from defiance. From watching someone else break free from the weight of tradition and deciding to do the same. From catching a glimpse of possibility—seeing that education isn't just a far-off dream reserved for others, but something real, something within reach. And sometimes, resilience comes from a quiet, unshakable truth: that even if the world refuses to believe in you, you can believe in yourself.

When I started working with GyaanJyoti, I thought role models were the celebrated figures whose names everyone recognized, the ones whose achievements are etched into history. But I've learned that role models are all around us, living quiet revolutions in ordinary lives. They are the girls who sit cross-legged on the floor of makeshift classrooms, their faces illuminated by the soft glow of a single bulb as they scrawl their dreams into the margins of tattered notebooks. They are the daughters who refuse to let their futures be written by the same hands that bound their mothers. They are the mothers who stand tall against generations of custom, declaring that their daughters will not stay home to cook and clean but will step into classrooms and rewrite their stories. They are the teachers who stay late into the night, fighting for every child, even when the odds seem insurmountable, even when no one is watching.

Role models are not always the ones who change the world in a sweeping, dramatic moment. They are the ones who plant seeds of change in the smallest of actions, day by day, decision by decision. They are the ones who refuse to surrender to despair, who show those around them that progress is possible—not through grand speeches, but through persistence, grit, and hope. They prove that a different future can be imagined, and once imagined, it can be created.

In villages where daughters are often taught to lower their gaze, these role models are teaching them to look ahead. In communities where tradition can feel immovable, they are showing that change often starts with a single courageous step. And sometimes that step—taken in defiance of doubt, fueled by the belief that the future doesn't have to mirror the past—is enough to spark something unstoppable. These quiet victories ripple outward, creating waves of transformation.

This ripple effect is where true resilience is born—not in moments of grandeur but in the steady unrelenting fight to make tomorrow brighter than today. And nowhere is this ripple effect more apparent than in education.

The Ripple Effect: How One Girl's Education Changes an Entire Community

When we think of education, we often see it as personal—a girl learning, growing and building a better life for herself. But education doesn't stop at one person. It ripples outward, shaping families, communities, and entire societies in ways no one can fully predict.

I've seen this happen firsthand. Last summer, I visited a school where many of the girls were supported by GyaanJyoti scholarships. Their fathers had been invited to attend a session about the importance of education. At first, they stood at the back of the room, arms crossed, their expressions unreadable. Some looked tired, others simply uninterested. For most of them, education had never been a priority for their daughters—school was something that happened in the background, an obligation, not an opportunity.

Speaking to the girls of Savitri Bai Phule Balika Inter College, Greater Noida, where GyaanJyoti sponsors the education of 33 girls.

But as I spoke about the impact education had on real families—stories of girls who had gone on to earn an income, support their parents and change their futures—something shifted. One father came up to me after the session. He admitted that he had never truly considered education important for his daughter. But seeing her excitement, hearing the stories of girls like her who had broken the cycle of poverty, had made him rethink. He wasn't fully convinced, not yet. But he was considering it. And sometimes, that's how change begins. Not in one grand moment, but in the small cracks that appear in old ways of thinking.

These small shifts don't just affect one household. When a father starts to believe in his daughter's education, his neighbors start to pay attention. When a girl stays in school and later contributes to her household income, other families start to wonder if maybe they should allow their daughters to study, too. The effect is slow but undeniable. The more girls who receive an education, the more families begin to see its worth.

And these changes don't stop at individual families—they reshape entire communities. An educated girl grows into a woman who earns an income, who makes decisions, who ensures her own children get an education. Over time, this cycle builds into something bigger than one generation. Schools that were once empty of girls start to fill up. Families that once hesitated now insist their daughters complete their studies. The same fathers who once questioned education start encouraging other parents to send their daughters to school. It may begin with a single girl, but soon, it is no longer just about her. It is about a collective shift, a transformation in what a community believes is possible.

This isn't just a theory—it's backed by real data. Studies show that when more women are educated, entire economies grow. Educated women tend to earn higher incomes, which they reinvest into their families. They ensure their children go to school, breaking cycles of poverty that have lasted for generations. Countries with higher female literacy rates have lower crime rates, stronger public health, and more stable economies. The numbers prove it—but so do the stories I've witnessed.

At GyaanJyoti, I've met girls who became the first in their families to finish school. Some of them went on to higher studies, while others used their education to start small businesses. One girl, who had once been discouraged from attending school, now runs a tutoring center in her village, helping younger students who might have otherwise dropped out. Another completed her education and convinced her parents to let her younger sisters do the same. These stories are proof that education isn't an isolated event—it is a force that spreads, growing stronger with each girl who is given the chance to learn.

In Dubai, education is taken for granted. No one questions whether a girl should go to school. It's a given, an expectation. But in so many parts of India, it's still a debate. It's still a choice that some families hesitate to make. But when they see the proof—when they see a girl succeed, contribute, and thrive—that hesitation starts to disappear. A community that once resisted change begins to embrace it. And over time, the belief that education is a privilege begins to shift into the understanding that it is a right.

And that's what keeps me going—because I know that every girl who gets an education isn't just changing her own life; she's changing the way an entire community thinks. She's shifting expectations. She's making it easier for the next girl to follow in her footsteps. And once that cycle starts, it doesn't stop. The ripples spread, reaching places no one thought possible—rewriting futures, one girl at a time. What starts with one girl's education eventually reshapes the course of a village, a town, a generation. And when that happens, it is no longer a ripple—it is a wave of change, too powerful to be turned back.

The Scale of Change We Can Create

It's easy to think of change as something distant—something that happens somewhere else, to someone else. But when you break it down, change is nothing more than a series of choices, small shifts that build on one another until the old way of thinking is replaced by something new. And at the heart of it all is a question: What happens when those choices are denied to half the population?

In so many ways, we've been conditioned to think of progress in numbers. How many girls enrolled in school this year? How many graduated? How many families moved out of poverty because their daughters got an education? These statistics are important—they help us see patterns, measure growth, and prove that we are moving forward. But what they don't capture are the moments that truly define change.

A father who once laughed at the idea of educating his daughter now proudly watches her leave for college. A mother who never had the chance to hold a pencil makes sure her daughter does her homework every evening. A girl who was expected to drop out and get married decides she will finish school, not just for herself but for the younger girls who look up to her. None of these moments can be plotted on a graph, but they matter just as much—maybe even more.

When I think about the scale of this issue, I think about all the untapped talent in the world. What if half the world's doctors, teachers, engineers, and leaders never got the chance to exist? What if the solutions to some of our biggest global problems are locked away in the minds of girls who never got the chance to learn? Educating girls isn't just about giving them equal opportunities—it's about ensuring that the world has access to every mind capable of contributing something valuable.

Whenever I talk to someone who is indifferent to this issue—not actively against it, but also not concerned—I ask them to think about it personally. What if it were their own daughter? Their own sister? Wouldn't they want her to have every chance to succeed? Sometimes, people need to be reminded that these girls are not distant statistics—they are real people with dreams, talents, and the potential to change the world if given the chance.

But this issue isn't only about fairness or wasted potential. It is about economic progress, stability, and the kind of future we want to create. The data is undeniable—when more women are educated, economies grow, poverty rates drop, and families become healthier. Countries with higher female literacy rates experience lower crime, stronger political engagement, and better social outcomes. Yet, despite all the evidence, many societies still hesitate to fully invest in girls' education. The cost of inaction is too high, not just for the girls themselves, but for entire nations.

For me, this work doesn't end here. As I move towards the next chapter of my life—DP final year, university, career, the future—I know that education and empowerment will always be part of my path. My experiences with GyaanJyoti have shaped me in ways I never expected. I've realized that passion is not enough; real change comes from strategy, from understanding the systems that create these barriers and finding ways to dismantle them.

Studying Economics has given me a new lens to view this issue. It's not just about doing the right thing—it's about making smart decisions that benefit entire societies. When more women are educated, economies grow. More businesses are created. Poverty rates decline. Families become healthier. Communities become stronger. Education is not just about personal growth—it's about national development, long-term economic stability, and building a workforce that includes everyone. There is no downside to investing in girls education—it's one of the most effective ways to build a better world for everyone.

But what happens when education is seen as a battle instead of a birthright? When girls are forced to fight for something that should be guaranteed? That is the reality for so many. And it's a fight that should not be theirs alone. It is a collective responsibility to ensure that education is no longer a privilege, but a norm for every child, regardless of gender or background.

I know that my role in this fight will evolve. Maybe I won't always be volunteering on the ground, but I will always be part of the conversation. Whether through policy, mentorship, or funding scholarships, I will continue to contribute in whatever way I can. Because once you see the power of education—the way it transforms not just individuals but entire communities—you can't look away. It becomes a part of you.

And maybe that's the real question we should all be asking ourselves. Not whether change is possible but what we are willing to do to make it happen. Because if we only admire progress from a distance, without taking action, then we're only watching the world move forward without being part of the push.

If half the world is held back, the world itself will never move forward. And if we are the ones with the privilege to make a difference, then we also carry the responsibility to act.

It's not enough to recognize the importance of education. The real question is—what are we willing to do about it?

CHAPTER 6

Turning Privilege into Purpose

We've reached the final chapter, but the story—the journey of these girls, this movement, and everything we've explored—is far from over. In fact, it's only just beginning. The five chapters before this weren't merely stories; they were windows into lives that could have easily been ours with just a slight change in fate or opportunity. These narratives are not distant; they reflect a shared humanity that connects us all.

Writing this book has helped me articulate what privilege truly means—not as an abstract concept, but as a lived reality. I've seen it through the eyes of Sakshi, Varsha, Kalpana, and other girls whose circumstances differ from mine, yet whose dreams burn with the same intensity. Their aspirations—to learn, to succeed, to be seen—are universal.

In Sakshi's determination to defy expectations, in Varsha's quiet resilience, and in Kalpana's unwavering hope, there's a common thread: possibility in the face of hardship. These girls navigate systems of gender, caste, and class that limit opportunity, yet their strength challenges those limits.

Coming to the end of this book doesn't feel like closing a chapter. It feels like standing at a beginning—an invitation to understanding, to action, and to responsibility. This isn't just their story; it's ours.

When I started this journey, I thought privilege was something you either had or didn't—an invisible line between the "fortunate" and the "unfortunate." Growing up in Dubai, privilege was obvious but rarely talked about. Comfort was the norm. But some moments stood out: construction workers in the brutal summer heat, people juggling multiple jobs and sharing rooms, and trips to India where children sold trinkets and flowers at traffic lights while I carried a backpack full of books. I noticed these things, but they felt distant—until GyaanJyoti happened.

Meeting girls like Sakshi and Varsha made it personal. Sakshi's dream of becoming a police officer wasn't just about her—it was about her community. Her resilience was inspiring but also unsettling. Why should going to school be so hard for her? Why did my worries revolve around deadlines while hers were about whether she could attend class at all?

There was guilt at first—the kind that nags at you. But guilt doesn't build schools or create opportunities. It sits with you and convinces you that feeling bad is enough. It isn't. I've learned privilege isn't a burden—it's a tool. The question isn't "Why do I have this?" but "What can I do with it?"

I used to think making an impact required something big—a foundation, a speech. But the moments that stay with me are quieter: Once I asked a girl selling flowers at the roadside ,whether she goes to school and what is her favourite subject ? Her absolute surprise was evident that a stranger cared enough to ask about her choices. Varsha explaining how her dream of studying BCA wasn't just for her, but for girls after her. These aren't headline moments. But they're real. Change isn't always loud—it's often found in small acknowledgments.

Privilege is being able to dream without hearing "no." It's being given a voice that people listen to. When my mom pushed me into taking debate classes, I didn't see it then, but she was giving me a platform—a confidence many girls never get. Sakshi has that same fire, but her path is steeper. She's not asking for charity—she's asking for a fair chance.

It's overwhelming to think of how many girls are denied education—not because they lack ambition, but because someone decided they didn't need it. Once you hear these stories, you can't ignore them. Fathers who once dismissed their daughters' schooling now celebrate their achievements. Awareness like that changes you.

So what now? Awareness without action isn't enough. Not everyone will start an organization. But everyone can do something—mentor someone, challenge harmful beliefs, or rethink how you use your resources. Privilege isn't measured by what you have—it's what you do with it.

This chapter is called "Turning Privilege into Purpose" for a reason. Privilege is a starting point, not an endpoint. Purpose doesn't have to be big or public. Sometimes, it's as simple as asking someone what they dream about. Sometimes, it's standing up for someone when it's easier to stay quiet. Sometimes, it's speaking up—even if your voice shakes.

Reframing Privilege

Privilege isn't something I always understood—not entirely, anyway. Throughout this book, I've explored how it shows up in ways that aren't always obvious—and as I reach this final chapter, I realize privilege is more complex than I ever thought. For a long time, it felt like a word that belonged to other people— ultra rich business families living in Emirates Hills or those with yachts docked in Dubai Marina. Growing up, I thought privilege meant extravagance: flashy cars, designer clothes, weekend getaways to places with unpronounceable names. But privilege can be quieter. It's in freedom, so ordinary that it goes unnoticed—like having parents who attend your school meetings, the freedom to choose your career path, or the safety of walking to school without fear. It's the luxury of not having to think about survival while others spend their days worrying about clean water or how to pay next month's fees. Working with GyaanJyoti deepened that understanding. It reframed privilege not as something you own but as something you can use—or waste. And that choice, I've realized, is where purpose begins.

So I want to ask you: What parts of your life do you rarely think about because they seem so normal? When was the last time you considered the ease with which you attend school, choose what to eat, or even decide how to spend your free time? These everyday freedoms are privileges in themselves. Have you ever thought about how different your choices might be if survival, safety, or acceptance wasn't guaranteed? It's not about guilt—it's about awareness. Because once you see those privileges clearly, the real question becomes: how can you turn them into something that benefits someone else?

One of the biggest realizations came from an encounter that seemed ordinary at first. I was walking near a temple in India when I saw a girl selling flowers. My first instinct was to pull some coins from my bag and hand them over—a small act of kindness, I thought. But something made me pause. Instead, I bought a few flowers and asked her about her education. Her eyes widened, caught between surprise and uncertainty before she answered softly. That simple conversation stayed with me. No one had ever asked her that before. Most people asked her how much the flowers cost or haggled over the price, not what she dreamed of or what made her eyes light up. That moment taught me something important: privilege isn't just having the resources to help—it's having the choice to stop, listen, and make someone feel seen and heard.

As mentioned earlier, my mom forced me into taking debate classes when I was ten. I hated it at that time—the pressure to speak up, the nerves that twisted my stomach before competitions. Back then, it felt like a forced inconvenience.

Now, I see what she was doing. She wasn't just making me argue over topics I didn't care about; she was teaching me how to use my voice. That's a privilege too—the privilege of being heard, of being taught that your words carry weight. Girls like Sakshi have that same fire, but they fight to be heard in rooms where their voices are often dismissed. My mom handed me a microphone; Sakshi had to fight for hers.

But here's something I hadn't considered before: privilege isn't something you keep. It's something you pass on. It's like standing at the edge of a river with a bridge under your feet. You didn't build that bridge, but you can help someone else cross it. The real question is: how are you using yours? I've come to realize that small choices carry weight—what we pay attention to, how we speak to people, and where we spend our money. I think about the times I've spent more on a meal in Dubai than it costs to fund a girl's education for a week. Those realizations sting, but they push me to be more conscious of my choices.

And here's another thing: doing nothing is also a choice. A comfortable one, but a choice nonetheless. Ignoring what you've seen doesn't make the world fairer—it just allows inequality to persist unchallenged. I've learned that awareness isn't enough; it's what you do with that awareness that matters. Privilege gave me a platform. But real change happens when we use it to amplify voices that have long gone unheard.

It's easy to believe that big actions are what make a difference. But change often starts with conversations that seem too small to matter—asking a flower-seller about her favorite subject, listening to a girl like Varsha talk about her dreams, or challenging someone when they say, "That's just how things are."

Privilege, I've learned, is not measured by how much you have. It's measured by what you choose to do with it.

Amplifying Voices

If I could sit down with the version of myself who began this journey—the girl who thought making an impact required bold, sweeping gestures—I'd have a lot to say. I'd tell her, "You don't need to have all the answers. You don't need to change everything overnight. And you definitely don't have to do it alone."

When I first got involved with GyaanJyoti, I thought making a difference meant having the perfect plan, leading some major initiative, or achieving something that looked impressive from the outside.

I believed that if my actions weren't big, they weren't enough. But reality has a way of softening those rigid beliefs. Change, I've learned, doesn't come from trying to be a hero— it comes from listening, showing up, and being present even when you're not sure what to say or do.

That's been one of the hardest lessons for me: understanding that mistakes aren't signs of failure—they're part of the process. There were times I said the wrong thing or felt paralyzed by how enormous the challenges seemed. I'd get caught in spirals of doubt, wondering if I was doing enough or if I was even the right person to help. But every time I met girls like Sakshi, Varsha, Kajal, Priyanka and Kalpana—girls whose courage outshone their circumstances—I was reminded that the point isn't perfection. It's persistence. Resilience isn't about never stumbling. It's about choosing to get back up, even when you're unsure of the road ahead.

One of the moments that shifted my perspective happened at a GyaanJyoti event. There was a girl sitting at the edge of the group, so quiet that it would've been easy to overlook her. I found myself drawn to her silence—the kind that felt heavy, like words left unsaid. I sat beside her, unsure of how to start a conversation, and finally asked, "What's your favorite subject?" Her hesitation was palpable, but after a pause, she whispered, "Math." Her face changed—not dramatically, but enough to notice. There was a flicker of pride, a subtle but unmistakable glow that comes from being acknowledged. Months later, I learned she'd convinced her parents to let her stay in school. It wasn't some large-scale initiative or a viral campaign that changed her trajectory— maybe a single conversation was the trigger point. That realization has stayed with me: never underestimate the power of making someone feel seen.

Before this journey, I thought activism looked like fiery speeches, crowded rallies, or holding up signs in protest. Those things matter, of course. But, real change often unfolds quietly. It's in the late-night conversations, the patient listening, and the willingness to ask uncomfortable questions and sit with the answers. Advocacy doesn't always come with a spotlight—it's found in the everyday choices we make. It's in sharing a meal with someone and asking how they're doing or taking the time to hear a story without interrupting to offer solutions. True change is measured not by how visible your actions are but by how deeply they touch the people you're trying to help.

I think back to my early days with GyaanJyoti, when I believed I had to be the one making the biggest difference. But I've since learned that meaningful impact is rarely about individual heroics. It's about collaboration, about joining hands with people who know their communities far better than I do. Real solutions don't come from swooping in with answers— they come from listening to those living the reality every day. That's what I admire most about the work GyaanJyoti does: it doesn't impose solutions. It empowers families to be part of their children's educational journeys. Because change rooted in dignity and partnership lasts far longer than change born of charity.

There's something deeply humbling about realizing how often we overlook the power of our everyday interactions. How many times do we walk past someone without really seeing them? How often do we assume that big gestures are the only ones that count? I've come to believe that some of the most important work happens in those moments that don't make headlines. The world shifts in small, deliberate ways—in conversations at dusty classrooms, in quiet nods of understanding, in the spark that lights up a girl's face when someone asks her what she dreams of becoming. That's the work that endures.

If I could share one lesson from this journey, it's this: you don't need a grand platform to make a difference.

You don't have to wait for the perfect moment or the ideal circumstances. Change begins in the choices you make when no one is watching. It starts with how you treat people, how you listen, how you use your voice—not to speak over others, but to uplift those who've long been unheard.

So I'll ask you, just as I've asked myself: When was the last time you listened—truly listened—to someone whose life looks nothing like yours? When was the last time you asked someone what they dream of and waited for the answer without rushing to fill the silence? Privilege isn't meant to be a shield that protects us from discomfort. It's meant to be a tool—a bridge to pull others closer, not push them away.

Personal impact is powerful, yes. But imagine if every conversation, every small act of kindness, every quiet gesture of acknowledgment could multiply beyond us. What if the real measure of privilege isn't how far you can go, but how many people you bring with you? That's a question I still carry with me, one I hope you'll carry too.

Scaling the Effort

If I've learned anything through this journey, it's that awareness isn't enough—it's what you do with that awareness that counts. Personal impact matters, but real, lasting change requires scaling those efforts beyond ourselves. And that's where things get complicated. You can reach one girl, you can change one family's perspective, but what happens when you want to reach hundreds? Thousands? How do you grow something as personal and relationship-driven as this work without losing the very heart that makes it effective?

I used to think the answer was simple: more money, more resources. And while funding matters, it's not the biggest hurdle. If I had unlimited resources, I wouldn't start by building more schools or handing out scholarships. Those are important—but they're not enough. The real challenge lies in changing mindsets. You can construct the most beautiful classrooms, but if people don't believe girls belong in them, those seats will stay empty. In many families, the decision isn't about affordability; it's about priorities. It's the belief that a son's education is an investment, while a daughter's is a luxury. Changing that thinking? That's the hard part—and the part no amount of funding can solve alone.

If I could implement one large-scale initiative, it would be a community advocacy program led by those who've lived it— former students who've succeeded through education going back to their villages to share their stories. I've seen firsthand how much more powerful a lived example is compared to any statistic. When a girl from a neighboring village stands up and says, "I studied, I work now, and I can support my family," it resonates in a way that numbers never could. Parents, especially fathers, start to listen when they see that educating their daughters isn't just the "right" thing to do—it's practical. It's an investment with real returns. Imagine workshops where these fathers sit together, hearing how daughters' incomes have lifted entire households out of poverty. Money speaks—but sometimes, stories speak louder. I've seen the way someone's face changes when they hear a story that hits close to home. Facts can be ignored; lived experiences are harder to dismiss.

And the conversation can't stop with academics.

If we're preparing girls for a future beyond traditional expectations, we need to show them what that looks like. Workshops focused on leadership, confidence, and long-term career goals aren't extras—they're essentials. So many girls I've met see education as a hurdle to clear before marriage, not a pathway to independence. We need to shift that narrative: finishing school isn't the end of the journey; it's the beginning of choices they didn't think they had. What if they saw women from similar backgrounds leading businesses, running clinics, or standing at the front of classrooms? Role models shouldn't feel like distant exceptions—they should be visible, relatable, and within reach.

But scaling change isn't just about what you do—it's about how you're received. Trust is the currency of this work. Families are often skeptical of NGOs. They wonder, "Why are you helping us? What's in it for you? Will this support disappear in a year?" I've seen how that skepticism can stall even the best-intentioned efforts. Relationships take time—there are no shortcuts. You have to show up consistently, with no hidden agendas. It means having uncomfortable conversations, respecting cultural nuances, and understanding that what works in one community may fail in another. Legal and bureaucratic roadblocks add another layer of complexity. Registering programs, and getting local approvals—these things can take months, sometimes years.

Change isn't slow only because people resist it; sometimes, the systems designed to facilitate progress end up delaying it. That kind of slow burn tests your patience, forcing you to confront how much you really believe in the work you're doing.

And then there's sustainability. It's easy to get caught up in the excitement of starting something new. Launch a program, get a few success stories, and celebrate. But what happens after the cameras are gone and the funding cycle ends? Real change sticks when local communities own the process. That means investing in local leadership, providing training, and ensuring that progress doesn't depend on a handful of outsiders. It's about building something that lasts long after people like me have moved on.

I've come to realize that it's less about being the person who makes things happen and more about making sure things keep happening—even when you're not there to witness it.

I won't lie—it's frustrating. There are days when the pace feels glacial, when setbacks make you wonder if it's worth it. I've become more impatient with excuses. When people shrug and say, "That's just how things are," I want to scream. Because I've seen how even the smallest actions can chip away at those old mindsets, but this work has also taught me patience. I used to believe that if you worked hard enough, change would come quickly. I thought that if you presented people with the right facts and the right stories, they'd immediately shift their views. But hearts and minds don't change on command. They shift gradually—sometimes so subtly you might not notice—until one day, a father who once dismissed his daughter's schooling is proudly bragging about her report card. Or a girl who never thought she'd make it past primary school is teaching a classroom full of students.

That duality—being impatient with the status quo while patient with the process—is something I wrestle with constantly. I've learned that change isn't a moment; it's a series of them, layered over time, often invisible until it becomes undeniable. And that's what keeps me going—the quiet knowledge that even if progress is slow, every small victory matters. Because the cost of inaction is far too high. Every year a girl is kept out of school, her opportunities shrink, and her world narrows. And when millions of girls are denied education, it's not just their future that's affected—it's all of ours. Economically, socially, and globally—when half the population is held back, everyone pays the price. I've studied enough economics to know that investing in girls isn't just a moral decision—it's a practical one. Countries with higher rates of female education have stronger economies, lower crime rates, and more stable governments. What if the solution to some of the world's biggest challenges is locked inside a mind we chose not to educate? That thought keeps me up at night.

And that's where you come in!

Scaling this effort isn't about a few people working tirelessly—it's about many people choosing to care, to act. Change on a large scale needs people like you. Not necessarily to start something new, but to support what's already working. To speak up in rooms where decisions are made, to challenge assumptions in everyday conversations, to donate if you can, volunteer if you have the time, or simply listen with an open heart. Solutions aren't built in isolation—they're created through collective effort, piece by piece, conversation by conversation.

What if you decided that the discomfort of seeing injustice was meant to push you toward action? What if, instead of thinking "someone else will handle it," you realized that someone could be you?

Change isn't waiting for the perfect moment. It's happening right now—through the choices we make, the voices we amplify, and the people we decide to stand with.

The question isn't whether you can make a difference.

It's whether you will.

Turning Awareness into Action

So, where do you begin?

The truth is, you don't need to uproot your life or launch a massive initiative to start making an impact. You begin where you are, with what you have. Start by listening. It sounds simple—maybe even too simple—but it's often overlooked. When was the last time you asked someone, really asked, about their struggles and let them speak without interruption or judgment? There's a difference between hearing and listening. Listening means setting aside assumptions and allowing someone else's reality to expand your own understanding. Change starts with conversations, and sometimes, those conversations happen in the most unexpected places—a bus ride, a grocery store line, a school hallway. It begins with caring enough to ask and being patient enough to hear.

If you're wondering what comes after listening, look at your everyday life. Do you have access to education? Offer to mentor someone who doesn't. Are you financially comfortable? Even a small, consistent donation to a grassroots organization like GyaanJyoti can change the trajectory of a child's future. These aren't hypothetical suggestions—they're real, actionable steps. You don't need a massive following or a fancy title. Use what's in front of you. Can you spare an hour a week to help a student with homework? Can you share a scholarship opportunity on your social media? Every action—no matter how small—adds up. A single textbook, a shared resource, or even a conversation that helps someone see their own potential can have ripple effects that extend far beyond what you'll ever see firsthand.

But here's something I've come to realize: good intentions aren't enough. Sometimes, well-meaning people rush to "fix" things without understanding what's actually needed. I've seen it happen—people donate resources without asking if those are the resources communities need. Or they assume throwing money at a problem will solve it. Money helps, sure. But it's not a cure-all. You can build a school, but if the community doesn't believe in educating their daughters, those classrooms will stay empty. That's why the first step isn't action—it's understanding. Listen first. Learn second. Act third. Anything else risks being more about easing your conscience than creating lasting change.

And let's talk about the savior complex—the idea that you're "saving" someone.

People aren't projects. They don't need saving. They need support, respect, and access to opportunities. The girls I've met through GyaanJyoti aren't sitting around waiting for someone to rescue them. They're working hard, fighting for their education, and navigating challenges most of us can't even fathom. They don't need heroes—they need allies. There's a difference. A hero swoops in, fixes things, and leaves. An ally stands beside you, listens to you, and helps you build something sustainable. So before you act, ask yourself: "Am I centering myself in this, or am I genuinely supporting what the community wants?" The goal isn't to lead every effort—it's to amplify the voices already doing the work.

Sometimes, the biggest impact you can make is closer to home than you think. Look around your local community. Is there a student who needs tutoring? A school that lacks resources? Change doesn't have to be global to be meaningful. The small actions—buying school supplies for a local child, helping someone fill out college applications, offering to listen when someone needs a safe space—those are the building blocks of bigger movements. Change is personal before it's ever political. And those personal actions? They matter.

But here's the part that stings: doing nothing is also a choice.

And that choice has consequences.

When you stay silent in the face of inequality, you're not just standing still, you're allowing the status quo to prevail. Silence is never neutral; it's a choice that echoes through systems and communities, perpetuating harm. And when you turn away because the problem feels too overwhelming, you place the weight of that burden on someone else—often those already carrying the heaviest loads.

Ask yourself: "Is the world I find comfortable today the world I want to pass on tomorrow?" Comfort can be deceiving. It can soothe us, lull us into inaction, or it can confine us, trapping us in a bubble of privilege and ignorance. The discomfort you feel when confronted by injustice isn't an enemy—it's a compass. It's there to wake you up and point you toward what needs your voice, your effort, and your action.

Every culture, every society, has its comfort zones—norms, traditions, and unspoken rules about who holds power and who remains unheard. Disrupting those patterns can feel destabilizing, even dangerous. But history shows us that every movement for justice began with people willing to lean into that discomfort. Whether it's the voices that refused to be quiet in the fight for civil rights, the courage of those marching for women's equality, or the resilience of Indigenous communities protecting their sacred lands; change has always been sparked by those who chose action over apathy.

And if you don't know where to begin, begin by caring. Caring is not passive—it's a powerful first step. Caring creates curiosity, and curiosity opens the door to understanding. Understanding leads to empathy, and empathy turns into meaningful, intentional action. It's a ripple effect, one that grows stronger when more people join in.

Not everyone can lead the protest, draft the legislation, or start the movement. But everyone can amplify the message, question harmful systems, and challenge the small injustices that appear in daily life. Change doesn't require perfection—it requires participation. And when enough people decide to do something, even if it's small, those ripples turn into waves. That's when change stops being an abstract ideal and becomes a living, breathing reality that transforms communities, cultures, and futures.

So listen to that discomfort. Let it fuel your questions, your actions, and your hope. This work isn't ending for me—and it doesn't have to end for you either.

The world isn't waiting for a hero. It's waiting for people who refuse to look away.

As Barack Obama rightly says -

"Change will not come if we wait for some other person or some other time.
We are the ones we've been waiting for. We are the change that we seek."

A Vision for the Future

When I first began this journey, I thought that creating change meant doing something big, something extraordinary. I believed that to make an impact, I had to figure it all out, have a perfect plan, and execute it flawlessly. But standing here now, at the end of this book and the beginning of what comes next, I realize that I had it backward. Change isn't about sweeping gestures or waiting for the right moment. It's about starting where you are, doing what you can, and trusting that those actions, no matter how small, matter. I started out thinking I needed to change the world. I've learned that it's about changing what's right in front of you—and believing that those ripples will spread.

I think back to all the girls I have come across due to my association with GyaanJyoti, I remember their smiles, their stories, their determination. I remember the quiet moments: sitting under a tree after a school event, laughing over shared snacks, exchanging dreams like they were secrets too precious to say aloud. I remember how Kalpana once whispered that she wanted to be a teacher so that other girls in her village would believe they could be more. I remember the shock on a young girl's face when I asked her what did she like doing the most in school, as if no one had ever thought to wonder. These stories aren't abstract. They are real, they are personal, and they are why I can't look away.

Once you've seen that spark of possibility in someone's eyes, it stays with you.

This work has changed me in ways I never expected. I used to hesitate before speaking up, worried I didn't know enough or wasn't qualified to say something. Now, I understand that silence is a choice—and one I'm no longer willing to make. I've learned that privilege isn't something to carry with guilt, but something to use responsibly. I've become more aware of how often inequality hides in plain sight, in the assumptions we make, and the opportunities we take for granted. This journey has taught me that action and awareness go hand in hand. Awareness without action can be a trap, making you feel like knowing is enough. It isn't. Knowing should lead to doing.

And yet, despite all the challenges I've witnessed, I feel hopeful. Hope isn't blind optimism. It's the belief that change is possible, backed by the work to make it real.

I've seen firsthand that when a girl is given an education, her world expands. Her family benefits, her community shifts, and generations are impacted. That kind of transformation is powerful. It's why I can't walk away from this work—and why I don't want to.

Looking ahead, I know that no matter where life takes me—whether it's into economics, policy, business, or something I haven't even imagined yet—education will remain at the core of what I do. I want to be part of creating long-term solutions, not just temporary fixes. That means working on policies that break down barriers, supporting organizations that listen to the communities they serve, and using my voice to spark conversations that matter.

Because change isn't just about programs and policies—it's about people. It's about asking ourselves, every day, how we can show up for others and what kind of world we want to help build.

What role will you play? What if your actions are the reason a girl stays in school or the bridge between someone's dream and their reality? These questions are not hypothetical—they're an invitation. An invitation to step in, stand up, and believe in what you can offer. Because you can make a difference.

None of us can do everything, but all of us can do something. And when enough people decide to act, to care, to refuse to look away, change becomes reality. This isn't the end of the journey—it's the beginning.

The book may close here, but the story continues.

The question is: Now that you know, what will you do?

Change doesn't start with "someone else."

It starts with you.

"I am only one, but I am one.

I cannot do everything, but I can do something.

And I will not let what I cannot do interfere with what I can do."

— EDWARD EVERETT HALE

My name is Kirti. My father name is Mr. Ashok Kumar. He is a security guard. My mother name is Ruby. She is housewife. Now I am in BA final year. I am doing my graduation from kurukshetra Univerity. I have completed by Schooling from Gout. Girl Sen. Sec School Model Town Panipat. I got 90% marks in 10th examination and 96% marks in 12th examination. I have been taking Scholarship from Gyan Jyoti since 9th class. Gyan Jyoti always motivated me and help me financially. I feel very proud that I am associated with Gyan Jyoti. Its play a important role in my life. With the help of Gyan Jyoti I can study freely and achieved good marks. I wont to become IAS offical. This exam is very difficult for all the people those who are not financially strong. But Gyan Jyoti always motivated me that You can clear exam with the help of hardwork and firm determination. Mr. Harish sir used to come my school and all other member of gyan Jyoti said to me that You can clear the exam. Mrs komal mam helps me alot after my schooling. Mrs komal mam help me to admission in kurukshetra Chiverity. and she also give

my admission fees and Hostel fees I really
want to thank to Mrs Komal mam
thatz believe me alot that I can clear
the exam.

मैं भी चाहती हूँ कि जब भी मैं कुछ बन जाऊ तो
मैं ज्ञान ज्योति की ही तरह गरीब लड़कियों की सहायता
करूं। ज्ञान ज्योति ऐसे ही गरीब लड़कियों की सहायता
करते रहे। ताकि हमारा देश ऐसे ही आगे बढ़ता रहे।
क्योंकि अगर एक लड़की पढ़ती है तो वह दो
घरों को संभालती है।

अंत में अपने शब्दों को विराम देते हुए मैं बिल से ज्ञान
ज्योति के सभी सदस्यों को धन्यवाद देना चाहती हूँ।
भगवान करे ज्ञान ज्योति ऐसे ही कार्य करता रहे।

Kirti

Kirti's story of resilience and her willingness to pay it forward.

Appendix: Lighting the Way - The Story of GyaanJyoti

As I reach the end of this book, I keep thinking about everything this journey has been—not just mine, but the stories I've had the privilege to witness and share. The names, the faces, the quiet moments of resilience—they don't leave you. They stay, reminding you that once you know, you can't unknow. Once you see, you can't look away.

Throughout this book, you've read about girls like Kajal and Priyanka. You've seen how education doesn't just change a classroom—it changes lives, families, and entire communities. And woven through those stories has been the presence of GyaanJyoti. Not as some distant organization, but as a collective of people who chose to act, to care, to show up.

GyaanJyoti wasn't built by any one person. It came to life in 2015 because a group of people believed that every girl deserves the chance to learn. What started with 32 girls, through friends and family has now reached 775 girls in the academic year 2024-25, being supported by GyaanJyoti. Those aren't just numbers. They're dreams rekindled, fears replaced with hope, and futures no longer defined by what's missing, but by what's possible.

I've seen it firsthand—how a simple act of support can change the way a girl sees herself. How having someone believe in you can be the difference between giving up and pushing forward. That's what GyaanJyoti stands for. Not charity. Not pity. Belief. Partnership. Possibility.

Their vision is simple:

Education of the girl child should never be a last priority. It's her right—something every child must have.

Their mission? To ensure no girl stands in the dark without someone lighting the path ahead:

To banish darkness from her life.

To enable her to carve her fate.

To help her see the life ahead.

To make her ready for every challenge.

Let us light a lamp of GyaanJyoti in her life.

And at its heart, the trust operates on values that are easy to say but harder to live by:

Integrity. Honesty. Transparency.

It's why every sponsorship goes directly to the girl's bank account, why the focus isn't just on paying fees but on standing beside her—through doubts, through setbacks, through the small wins that lead to bigger ones.

Over time, GyaanJyoti has grown beyond its beginnings, opening new chapters in Greater Noida, Ashiana (Bhiwadi, Rajasthan), and near Gurgaon. With each step, they've proven that change doesn't need to be complicated—it just needs commitment.

Here's a look at how it all comes together:

And that's the thing about stories like these—they don't really end. They continue in classrooms where girls raise their hands a little higher. In families where a daughter's dream becomes something everyone starts believing in. In communities where the idea of 'what's possible' keeps expanding, stories like Kirti's show us how far determination and support can go.

Kirti's story is one of those sparks that keeps the light spreading. Like so many others, she grew up knowing that education wasn't always a given. But with GyaanJyoti's support, she turned that uncertainty into determination. She worked tirelessly, securing 90% in her 10th and 96% in her 12th grade exams, and she is now in her final year of a BA at Kurukshetra University. More than just financial aid, what she found through GyaanJyoti was the strength to keep going—to believe in her dreams, even when the road ahead seemed unclear.

Now, as she sets her sights on becoming an IAS officer, Kirti carries forward the same values that once shaped her own path. She doesn't just want to succeed—she wants to give back, to stand behind someone else the way GyaanJyoti stood behind her. In her own words, she shares what this journey has meant to her.

This isn't about doing everything. It's about doing what you can. Maybe that's choosing to stand behind someone's dream. Maybe it's remembering that small steps, taken consistently, can move mountains.

The light spreads—one person, one act, one belief at a time.

And sometimes, being part of that is simpler than you think.

To learn more about GyaanJyoti and how you can support their work, visit their official website: *www.gyaanjyoti.com.*

GYAANJYOTI MODEL

Reducing Drop out Rates at Schools & Encouraging higher education for underprivileged Girls

www.gyaanjyoti.com

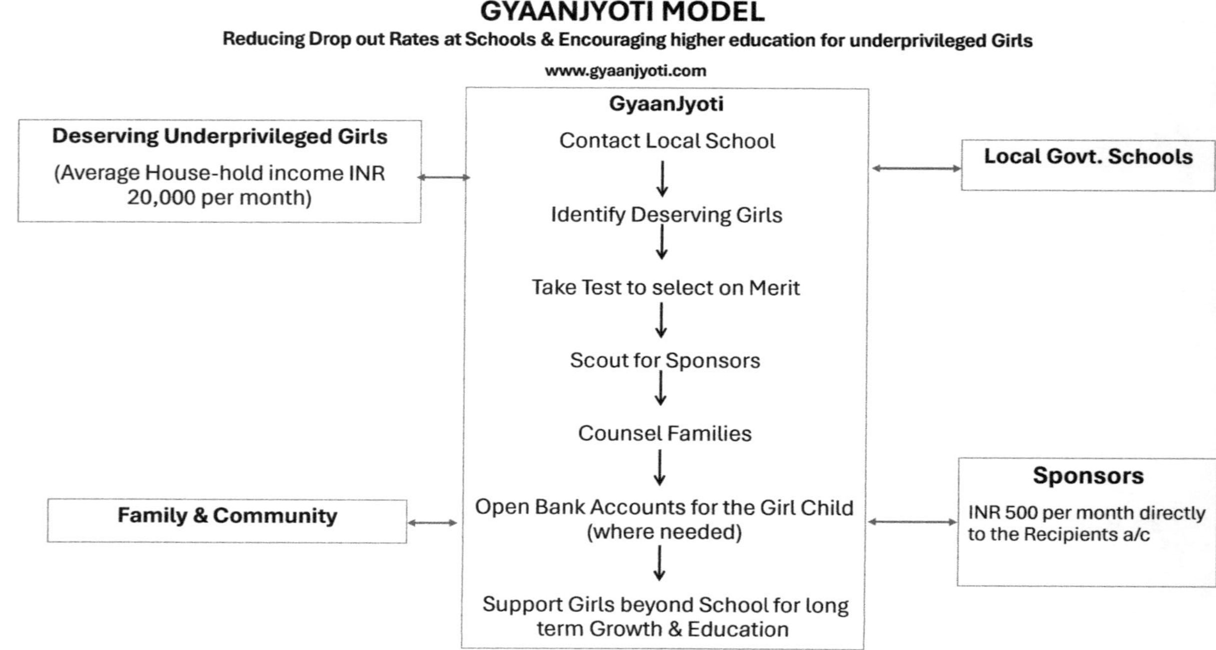

Author Bio

Avni is a teen author who believes stories connect us, challenge us, and change the way we see the world. Whether through debating, reading, or listening to people's experiences, she's always been drawn to voices that deserve to be heard—especially those of girls who fight for an education against the odds and dream beyond what's expected of them.

Inspired by figures like Malala Yousafzai, Avni views education as a lifeline. Writing this book was her way of sharing the hope and determination she witnessed firsthand—stories that stayed with her and made her question how easily we overlook others' realities.

Avni loves reading biographies and autobiographies of inspiring strong women role models, playing tennis, enjoys deep-sea diving and engaging in thoughtful debates with her friends. She enjoys exploring new ideas and believes that change begins by asking the right questions and listening carefully to others.

Her greatest hope is that this first book of hers makes you think, feel, and see things a little differently. If these stories linger or spark reflection, that's reason enough for her to have written it.